In Accordance with the Scriptures

The Didsbury Lectures
Series Preface

The Didsbury Lectures, delivered annually at Nazarene Theological College, Manchester, are now a well-established feature on the theological calendar in Britain. The lectures are planned primarily for the academic and church community in Manchester but through their publication have reached a global readership.

The name "Didsbury Lectures" was chosen for its double significance. Didsbury is the location of Nazarene Theological College, but it was also the location of Didsbury College (sometimes known as Didsbury Wesleyan College), established in 1842 for training Wesleyan Methodist ministers.

The Didsbury Lectures were inaugurated in 1979 by Professor F. F. Bruce. He was followed annually by highly regarded scholars who established the series' standard. All have been notable for making high calibre scholarship accessible to interested and informed listeners.

The lectures give a platform for leading thinkers within the historic Christian faith to address topics of current relevance. While each lecturer is given freedom in choice of topic, the series is intended to address topics that traditionally would fall into the category of "Divinity." Beyond that, the college does not set parameters. Didsbury lecturers, in turn, have relished the privilege of engaging in the dialogue between church and academy.

Most Didsbury lecturers have been well-known scholars in the United Kingdom. From the start, the college envisaged the series as a means by which it could contribute to theological discourse between the church and the academic community more widely in Britain and abroad. The publication is an important part of fulfilling that goal. It remains the hope and prayer of the College that each volume will have a lasting and positive impact on the life of the church, and in the service of the gospel of Christ.

1979	Professor F. F. Bruce†	*Men and Movements in the Primitive Church*
1980	The Revd Professor I. Howard Marshall †	*Last Supper and Lord's Supper*
1981	The Revd Professor James Atkinson†	*Martin Luther: Prophet to the Church Catholic*
1982	The Very Revd Professor T. F. Torrance†	*The Mediation of Christ*
1983	The Revd Professor C. K. Barrett†	*Church, Ministry and Sacraments in the New Testament*
1984	The Revd Dr A. R. G. Deasley	*The Shape of Qumran Theology*
1985	Dr Donald P. Guthrie†	*The Relevance of John's Apocalypse*
1986	Professor Andrew F. Walls	*The Nineteenth-Century Missionary Movement*
1987	The Revd Dr A. Skevington Wood†	*Reason and Revelation*

"John Behr is quite exceptional among modern Orthodox theologians. His range is enormous—from exacting textual scholarship in editions of great patristic works, a major study of St. John's Gospel, to short, attractively presented works aimed at the general reader. Now, following the early fathers in drawing from the Scriptures, he presents a vision of Christ on the cross, in death giving birth to Christians—the children of the church as virgin mother."

—**Andrew Louth**, Professor Emeritus, Durham University

"John Behr has wrested Christian readers from habitually reverting to 'the Bible' as a linear sequence of discrete dispensational phases, beginning with creation, climaxing in Christ, and ending with the consummation. Behr asks us read the Scriptures 'apocalyptically' through the lens of the cross, with a view to an eschatological mystery still unfolding. Behr helps us to break through to a whole new vision of how the Scriptures form believers."

—**Paul M. Blowers**, Dean E. Walker Professor of Church History, Milligan University

"These lectures, which will not let us see the key terms of the gospel—Adam, Christ, life, death, virgin, church—in any light other than that of the cross, not only indicate a remarkable new depth and clarity in Behr's thought but also open a port of entry into the very heart of Christian theology, illuminating the wisdom and power of the Scriptures as they are unveiled by the death of Jesus Christ."

—**Chris E. W. Green**, Professor of Public Theology, Southeastern University

"Dietrich Bonhoeffer prefaced his lectures on Genesis with the words 'The church . . . reads the whole of Holy Scripture as the book of the end, of the new, of Christ.' With this new book, renowned patristic scholar and theologian John Behr brilliantly demonstrates Bonhoeffer's classic Christian hermeneutical maxim for theological interpretation. *In Accordance with the Scriptures* provides a handy, brief, and highly accessible summary of John's lifelong research into patristic Christ-centered exegesis and thus the very shape of Christian theology."

—**Jens Zimmermann**, J. I. Packer Chair of Theology, Regent College

1988	The Revd Professor Morna D. Hooker	*Not Ashamed of the Gospel: New Testament Interpretations of the Death of Christ*
1989	The Revd Professor Ronald E. Clements†	*Wisdom in Theology*
1990	The Revd Professor Colin E. Gunton†	*Christ and Creation*
1991	The Revd Professor J. D. G. Dunn†	*Christian Liberty: A New Testament Perspective*
1992	The Revd Dr Paul M. Bassett†	*The Spanish Inquisition*
1993	Professor David J. A. Clines†	*The Bible in the Modern World*
1994	The Revd Professor James B. Torrance†	*Worship, Community, and the Triune God of Grace*
1995	The Revd Dr R. T. France†	*Women in the Church's Ministry*
1996	Professor Richard Bauckham	*God Crucified: Monotheism and Christology in the New Testament*
1997	Professor H. G. M. Williamson	*Variations on a Theme: King, Messiah and Servant in the Book of Isaiah*
1998	Professor David Bebbington	*Holiness in Nineteenth Century England*
1999	Professor L. W. Hurtado†	*At the Origins of Christian Worship*
2000	Professor Clark Pinnock†	*The Most Moved Mover: A Theology of God's Openness*
2001	Professor Robert P. Gordon	*Holy Land, Holy City: Sacred Geography and the Interpretation of the Bible*
2002	The Revd Dr Herbert McGonigle†	*John Wesley*
2003	Professor David F. Wright†	*What Has Infant Baptism Done to Baptism? An Enquiry at the End of Christendom*
2004	The Very Revd Dr Stephen S. Smalley†	*Hope for Ever: The Christian View of Life and Death*
2005	The Rt Revd Professor N. T. Wright	*Surprised by Hope*
2006	Professor Alan P. F. Sell†	*Nonconformist Theology in the Twentieth Century*
2007	Dr Elaine Storkey	Sin and Social Relations
2008	Dr Kent E. Brower	*Living as God's Holy People: Holiness and Community in Paul*
2009	Professor Alan Torrance	*Religion, Naturalism, and the Triune God: Confronting Scylla and Charybdis*
2010	Professor George Brooke	*The Dead Sea Scrolls and Christians Today*
2011	Professor Nigel Biggar	*Between Kin and Cosmopolis: An Ethic of the Nation*
2012	Dr Thomas A. Noble	*Holy Trinity: Holy People: The Theology of Christian Perfecting*
2013	Professor Gordon Wenham	*Rethinking Genesis 1–11*
2014	Professor Frances Young	*Construing the Cross: Type, Sign, Symbol, Word, Action*
2015	Professor Elaine Graham	*Apologetics without Apology*
2016	Professor Michael J. Gorman	*Missional Theosis in the Gospel of John*
2017	Professor Philip Alexander & Professor Loveday Alexander	Priesthood and Sacrifice in the Epistle to the Hebrews
2018	Professor Markus Bockmuehl	The Four Evangelists on the Presence and Absence of Jesus
2019	Professor Michael Lodahl	*Matthew Matters*
2020	Professor John Swinton	*Deliver Us from Evil*

2021	Professor John Barclay	Beyond Charity: Rethinking Gift and Community with Paul
2022	Professor David Wilkinson	*How Does God Act in the World?*
2023	Professor Amos Yong	Jesus in Cartographic Perspective**
2024	Professor John Behr	*In Accordance with the Scriptures*

In Accordance with the Scriptures

The Shape of Christian Theology

THE DIDSBURY LECTURES

JOHN BEHR

CASCADE Books · Eugene, Oregon

IN ACCORDANCE WITH THE SCRIPTURES
The Shape of Christian Theology

The Didsbury Lectures Series

Copyright © 2025 John Behr. All rights reserved. Except for brief quotations in critical publications or reviews, no part of this book may be reproduced in any manner without prior written permission from the publisher. Write: Permissions, Wipf and Stock Publishers, 199 W. 8th Ave., Suite 3, Eugene, OR 97401.

Cascade Books
An Imprint of Wipf and Stock Publishers
199 W. 8th Ave., Suite 3
Eugene, OR 97401

www.wipfandstock.com

PAPERBACK ISBN: 979-8-3852-3081-5
HARDCOVER ISBN: 979-8-3852-3082-2
EBOOK ISBN: 979-8-3852-3083-9

Cataloguing-in-Publication data:

Names: Behr, John [author].

Title: In accordance with the Scriptures : the shape of Christian theology / by John Behr.

Description: Eugene, OR: Cascade Books, 2025 | Series: The Didsbury Lectures Series | Includes bibliographical references and index.

Identifiers: ISBN 979-8-3852-3081-5 (paperback) | ISBN 979-8-3852-3082-2 (hardcover) | ISBN 979-8-3852-3083-9 (ebook)

Subjects: LCSH: Theology, Doctrinal—History—Early church, ca. 30–600. | Jesus Christ—Person and offices. | Typology (Theology). | Bible—Criticism, interpretation, etc. | Bible—Inspiration. | Hermeneutics—Religious aspects—Christianity—History.

Classification: BT78 B447 2025 (paperback) | BT78 (ebook)

VERSION NUMBER 03/21/25

The image on the front cover is copyright Vatican Library, used with permission. Images on Plates 1–3, 5, 8–11, 13, 15 are from Wikimedia, used under Attribution-ShareAlike 4.0 International. Images 4 and 12, are copyright Genevra Kornbluth, used with permission. Image 7 used courtesy of Princeton Art Museum. Image 14 used courtesy of the Bodleian Library. Image 17, copyright Alamy, used with permission.

Some material in what follows is drawn from my earlier articles: in chapter 2 from, "'For This Reason the Father Loves Me': Drawing Divinity into Himself to Minister Divinity to Us," *International Journal of Systematic Theology* 25.1 (2023) 47–59 and "Speaking of Incarnation: Modern Predicaments and Ancient Paradigms," in *The God Who Is for Us: Explorations in Constructive Dogmatics*, edited by Oliver Crisp and Paul Nimmo. Scottish Dogmatics Conference Series. Grand Rapids: Zondervan, forthcoming 2025.

For John MacMurray, Paul Young, Kenneth Tanner, Cherith Fee-Nordling, Julie Canlis, Bradley Jersak, Chris E. W. Green, Brian Zahnd, Vassa Larin, and Douglas Campbell—the Open Table team—who have reinforced the truth, as Origen put it, that we should "above all things attend to the reading of the Scriptures."

Contents

List of Images / xi
Preface / xiii
Abbreviations / xv

Chapter 1. Figuring Scripture / 1
Chapter 2. The Paschal Christ / 28
Chapter 3. The Virgin Mother / 67
Chapter 4. Becoming Human / 93

Postscript / 123
Bibliography / 129
Index of Ancient Sources / 137
Index of Authors / 145

List of Images

1: The Crucifixion, Panel from the Doors of St Sabina, Rome, 430–432 CE
2: The Crucifixion, Panel from an Ivory Casket, British Museum, 420–430 CE.
3: The Crucifixion, Rabbula Gospels, Syria, sixth century.
4: The Crucifixion, detail from the Sancta Sanctorum reliquary box, Vatican Museum, Syria or Palestine, sixth century.
5: The Anastasis, Istanbul, Church in Chora, commissioned by Theodore Metochites, 1310–1317 CE.
6: The Anastasis (of Adam), the Chludov Psalter (Historical Museum, Moscow, ms. gr. 129, 63v), Byzantine, ninth century.
7: The Crucifixion and Resurrection, the Princeton Psalter (Ps 8:7–10, recto), 1090–1100.
8: The Nativity, marble relief on a gravestone at Sangri on Naxos (Byzantine Museum in Athens, BXM 312), ca. 400 CE.
9: The Adoration of the Magi, detail from a sarcophagus in the cemetery of St Agnes, Rome, fourth century.
10: The Adoration of the Magi, mosaic in the Basilica of Santa Maria Maggiore, Rome, ca. 435.
11: The Adoration of the Magi, ivory panel, British Museum, London (1904, 0702.1).
12: The Nativity of Christ, detail from the Sancta Sanctorum reliquary box, Vatican Museum, Syria or Palestine, sixth century.

List of Images

13: The Nativity of Christ, mosaic in the Church in Daphni, Greece, ca. 1100 CE.

14: The Crucifixion and Wound of Christ, The "Bohun Psalter and Hours," Bodleian Library MS. Auct. D. 4. 4, England, ca. 1370–1380.

15: The Nativity of Christ, Novgorod, 1500–1525.

16: The Anastasis and Holy Zion, the Chludov Psalter (Historical Museum, Moscow, ms. gr. 129, 100v), Byzantine, ninth century.

17: The Icon of the Virgin of the Passion (Amolyntos), Byzantine and Christian Museum, Athens, ca. 1610

18: The Virgin Kardiotissa, Angelos Akotantos, 1400–1450.

Preface

ALMOST TWENTY YEARS AGO, I published the book *The Mystery of Christ: Life in Death* (2006). It was my attempt to synthesize what I had learnt in preparing my two earlier volumes, *The Way to Nicaea* (2001) and *The Nicene Faith* (2004), working my way through the theological reflections of the first four centuries. Now, having produced editions and translations (with extensive introductions) of Origen's *On First Principles* (2017) and Gregory of Nyssa's *On the Human Image of God* (2023) as well as a full study of the Gospel of John (2019), it became clear to me that it was time to summarize again what I have since learnt of early Christian theology. The past two or three decades have, in many ways, been an experience of unlearning what I thought I knew about Christian theology as we tend to think of it today, that is, as structured around various fixed themes (the Trinity, creation, the fall, incarnation and Christology, salvation and ecclesiology, etc.). The figures I have been studying over the past decades did not think with these as determining categories, and the attempt to present their thinking around such themes undoes the vitality and freshness of their ways of thinking theologically and the way in which they bore witness to Christ in their own times. To hear their voices, rather than filter them through our own systems, is an arduous task; for me, it required patiently preparing editions and translations. Hopefully, this small volume will help open up their theological vision in ways that might let them speak again today, in an era where the discipline of theology has become increasingly fractured into numerous subdisciplines so that, too often, the center no longer holds or is even forgotten. I have had the opportunity to present parts of this volume in many locations around the world and am thankful for all the reactions I received, but I am especially thankful to the Nazarene

Preface

Theological College and community, who invited me to give the Didsbury Lectures for 2024, giving me an opportunity to pull my thoughts together into a unified set of lectures, now chapters, and to Robin Parry and Wipf & Stock for their work in seeing them through to publication.

The editions and translations of the ancient texts referred to in this study, together with their abbreviated titles, are listed in the bibliography. They have been cited according to book/chapter/paragraph, as appropriate, and when the text is not divided into chapters or paragraphs, I have used the names of the editor and translator followed by the page number. The translations have often been modified, sometime extensively.

References to the Psalms are given in the Hebrew numeration followed by the Septuagint (LXX).

The bibliography contains only those works cited in this volume.

Abbreviations

ACW	Ancient Christian Writers
ANF	Ante-Nicene Fathers
CCSG	Corpus Christianorum: Series Graeca
CTC	Christian Theology in Context
CWS	Classics of Western Spirituality
CSCO	Corpus Scriptorum Christianorum Orientalum
DOML	Dumbarton Oaks Medieval Library
FC	Fathers of the Church
GCS	Die griechische christliche Schriftsteller der ersten [drei] Jarhunderte
GNO	Gregorii Nysseni Opera
IJSCC	*International Journal for the Study of the Christian Church*
IJST	*International Journal of Systematic Theology*
JBL	*Journal of Biblical Literature*
JECS	*Journal of Early Christian Studies*
JR	*Journal of Religion*
JTS	*Journal of Theological Studies*
LCL	Loeb Classical Library
MTh.	*Modern Theology*
NPNF	Nicene and Post Nicene Fathers
OAF	Oxford Apostolic Fathers
OCT	Oxford Classical Texts
OECS	Oxford Early Christian Studies
OECT	Oxford Early Christian Texts
PPS	Popular Patristic Series
PG	Patrologia Graeca

Abbreviations

PTS	Patristiche Texte und Studien
RSR	*Recherches de Science Religieuse*
SA	Studia Anselmiana
SBL	Society of Biblical Literature
SC	Sources chrétiennes
Suppl. *VC*	Supplements to *Vigiliae Christianae*
TS	*Theological Studies*
VC	*Vigiliae Christianae*

1

Figuring Scripture

From "The Bible" to Scripture

IN HER WONDERFUL BOOK, *The Literary Imagination in Jewish Antiquity*, Eva Mroczek asks the provocative question: How did the world of Second Temple Judaism think about its literature "before the concepts of 'book' and 'Bible,' which structure our own literary imagination, were available to think with."[1] In a manner similar to Skinner's "mythology of doctrines,"[2] Mroczek argues that our deeply-ingrained, but culturally-conditioned, categories of "book" and, in religious contexts, "Bible" constrict and distort how we understand the world of Second Temple Judaism. Even to speak of "a proto-Bible" (or "proto-canon") is, she argues, misleading: "Instead, there is a different morphology of text, a different sense of where revelation is to be found and how it relates to the figures who transmit it."[3] Mroczek opens up for us a much more varied and fascinating world—one in which there was no such thing as a standardized Book of Psalms or Psalter and in which David wrote 4,050 psalms. She suggests that perhaps now, with the advent of digital texts, ones that are not bounded by physical covers, we can learn to hear again how the ancients spoke about their own texts, the metaphors they used, and the histories of texts they provided. Rather than "books," she claims, "writing was part of a heavenly archive never fully

1. Mroczek, *Literary Imagination*, ix.
2. Skinner, "Meaning and Understanding in the History of Ideas."
3. Mroczek, *Literary Imagination*, 186.

reflected in available texts: a perpetually evolving multigenerational work constantly adding new episodes."[4]

Whilst exploring the literary imagination of Second Temple Judaism, unbounded by the ideas of book or canon, or by the attempt to trace antecedents for these, Mroczek does, of course, acknowledge that soon after the beginning of the common era, the idea of canon and book took hold. "One of the major differences interpreters have identified as a dividing marker between Jewish and Christian theologies as they emerge in late antiquity," she writes, is that "in Jewish theology the divine is contained in Scripture, and in Christian, God is incarnate in the person of Jesus Christ."[5] This might sound straightforward enough, but that it immediately appears so should give caution. Mroczek repeatedly notes how the categories of "Bible" and "canon" are so deeply ingrained that even attempts to think beyond or before them (such as the "rewritten Bible" and "biblical interpretation") still ultimately work with them.

If this is true, it is equally true, or perhaps even more so, for the theological framework within which we think theology—not the abstract propositions themselves, but the way in which they are apprehended by our theological imagination, the different paradigms within which formulations take flesh. These are, in great part, shaped by the patterns we have inherited from the printed book that we know as "The Bible": the printed single volume, containing Old and New Testaments, beginning with Genesis and ending with Revelation. But this is, overstating it only slightly, the invention of the printing press. Certainly, there were the great codices produced in the fourth century, but these were few and far between (and expensive: Constantine himself provided for their production).[6] Moreover, these codices were not, in fact, representative of how most Christians encountered scripture. The usual collected form was (and liturgically still is) the lectionary: the *Prophetologion*, the *Apostolikon*, and the *Evangelion*, a fact made clear by the overwhelming number of such manuscripts compared to those of "The Bible," or even the New Testament, and which critical scholarship is only recently beginning to take into account.[7]

---

4. Mroczek, *Literary Imagination*, 18.

5. Mroczek, *Literary Imagination*, 186.

6. Eusebius, *Life of Constantine* 4.36; Louth, "Inspiration of the Scriptures," 32–33.

7. See Spronk et al., *Catalogue of Byzantine Manuscripts*, esp. 289–315. Compared to the relatively small number of Pandect Bibles (approximately 15), there are 1,796 Gospel lectionary codices, 1,726 tetraevangelia codices, 319 codices of the "Apostolos," and 51 codices containing the Gospels, Acts, and Apocalypse together.

The theological framework given to us by "The Bible," which is now simply assumed, can be represented in this figure:

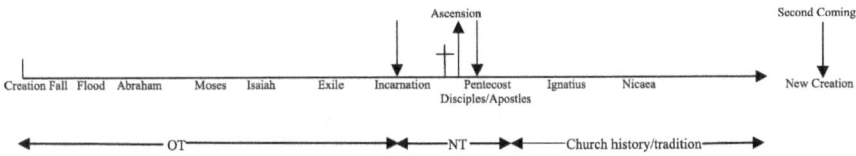

Figure 1

This is assumed to be the narrative arc for Christian theology: Creation–Fall–Salvation History–Incarnation–Crucifixion–Resurrection–Ascension–Pentecost, and, after the period covered by "The Bible," an onwards movement through history, culminating in the second coming and a new creation. There has been much debate, of course, over the past century or more, about whether Christ should be taken as the "mid-point" of history or whether "the Christ-event" constitutes the transition of the ages, either with the new age being inaugurated or apocalyptically breaking in from above. Whatever the variation on these themes, something like Figure 1 is assumed. Yet the implied historical arc of "The Bible" is not, of course, the historical order of the production of the books: historically, we instead have an unspecified, undelimited range of scriptures existing at the time of Jesus;[8] a couple of decades or so after the passion, Paul began to write his letters; and only then were the Gospels written. Figure 1 thus does not represent the historical order, nor the liturgical order (in which the reading from Scripture is followed by the Apostle, and only then the Gospel), nor, as we shall see, the hermeneutical order.

It should also be noted that the theological framework represented by Figure 1 is reinforced by our having inherited a fully fleshed-out liturgical calendar (in which, say, the feast of Christmas, the Nativity, is distinct from Pascha or Easter) so that the "incarnation" is thought of as the birth of Jesus from Mary, thirty-three years before the passion, with a distinct theological content, even though the classic work *On the Incarnation* was written by Athanasius before his liturgical calendar had a feast of the Nativity and despite his not mentioning Mary in his work—a work in which he intends, as

---

8. The accounts of the writings of these books are numerous. One may profitably consult Schniedewind, *How the Bible Became a Book* and *Who Really Wrote the Bible*.

we will see, to demonstrate that, in his words, "the One on the Cross is the Word of God" (*Gent.* 1), an order of identification that is not incidental. It took time, as Thomas Talley comments, for the "single mystery of redemption" to be refracted "into a series of commemorations of discrete historical moments in that mystery,"[9] from the observation of the feast of Pascha in a single night to a triduum comprising death, entombment, and resurrection, and then to a full liturgical calendar. If the feast of the Nativity was not part of the repertoire of theological thinking in an earlier age, assuming it when exploring the first centuries of Christian theological thinking can only lead to further anachronisms, as we will see in later chapters.

If we want to understand the genesis and coherence of Christian theology, we need to unmoor the hold that Figure 1 has on our theological imagination and open up an alternative framework or picture within which to undertake the task of attempting to understand the revelation of God in Christ, the last Adam (and, in turn, the first Adam), and, indeed, ourselves.

The plotting of the narrative in Figure 1, begins, of course, with what is assumed to be at the beginning—creation and Adam, then a fall from immortal life into death—and ends with, or has as a midpoint in, Christ, with the sequence of Incarnation-Cross-Resurrection-Ascension-Pentecost. However, when the correlation between Adam and Christ was first drawn by Paul, he was not drawing upon a settled and recognized picture of Adam and the fall; he was, rather, significantly recasting the figure of Adam. John Levison points out that "portraits of Adam in Early Judaism are characterized more by diversity than unity. The diversity is due to the incorporation of the Genesis narrative into the *Tendenzen* of individual authors."[10] There were, he continues, three commonalities in the way wisdom authors utilize the texts of Genesis 1:26–28 and 2:7. First, as an encouragement to pursue wisdom; second, depicting Adam as one who lacked wisdom; and, strikingly, third, "they include no references to the transgression of Adam and its effect because they regard death and the difficulties of life as natural phenomena which characterize the totality of human existence." It is only with the late 4 Ezra and 2 Baruch that "the extent of the effects of Adam's sin" is probed, with the idea that "his transgression brings physical difficulties and death into the present age." Yet, of course, 4 Ezra and 2 Baruch are universally held to be later than Paul, so they do not provide an explanation or background for Paul's thought; it is more likely that they were influenced

---

9. Talley, *Origins of the Liturgical Year*, 39.
10. Levison, *Portraits of Adam in Early Judaism*, 159.

by Paul's novel use of Adam. Even more strikingly, James Barr argues that Genesis presents a very different picture than is usually presumed:

> Adam and Eve were not immortal beings who by sin fell into a position where they must die; they were mortal beings who had a remote and momentary chance of eternal life but gained this chance only through an act of their own fault, and who because of that same act were deprived of that same chance.[11]

He continues later on:

> Large elements of the text [of Genesis] cannot be made to support Paul's use of the story without distortion of their meaning. . . . Paul was not interpreting the story in and for itself; he was really *interpreting Christ* through the use of images from this story.[12]

Although Barr assumes that Paul did indeed have an idea of what we have come to think of as "the fall," his point that Paul drew upon scripture to interpret Christ is an important insight and one that provides an entry into an alternative (and earlier) theological framework.

Paul, however, was not the only one not to assume the theological framework imposed by the structure of "The Bible" (Figure 1). While the background for Paul's Adam/Christ parallel and contrast has primarily been sought in Second Temple texts (and it is not there), there were other writers who also didn't assume "The Bible" and its implied framework, ones who might provide a way of understanding Paul and the proclamation of the gospel in ways other than those to which we have become accustomed: specifically, figures such as Irenaeus and Origen (together with later writers), figures who are too often left aside in examining such matters (presumably because it is assumed that we already know how they think—along the lines of Figure 1). Yet they also lived in the period before "The Bible" became a book, and their ways of thinking about scripture are not captive to our presuppositions. As we will see, when we remove the hold that Figure 1 has over our imagination and return to early Christians, such as Irenaeus and Origen, we find a very different way of configuring scripture and theology and understanding their coherence.

---

11. Barr, *Garden of Eden*, 21.
12. Barr, *Garden of Eden*, 89, italics original.

In Accordance with the Scriptures

Scripture as a Field of Literature

Rather than thinking about scripture as a bound book, with two testaments (or bodies) of literature and a canonical listing and order, it is better to think of scripture as a field of literature, with certain texts being more central (such as Genesis, Exodus, Isaiah, Psalms, etc.) and others more marginal (e.g., Bel and the Dragon), with different versions of the same texts, different collections of texts within "books" (e.g., Psalms), and many different ways of reading these texts. This can perhaps be represented as a circle: a field of scriptural literature.

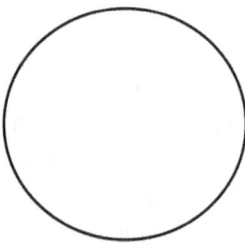

Figure 2

Depicting this as a circle is not meant to curtail or restrict the scope to a bounded collection. In fact, in the early centuries, the extent of the literature to be counted as scripture was not *the* central concern of early Christianity (no council, for instance, was called to determine a list), nor was their "order" (as presumed by "canonical criticism"): the canon is the canon of truth/faith, not a list. Certainly, by the time of Irenaeus, the four Gospels had become traditional, and so, too, the letters of Paul, but this was more a matter of traditioning rather than deliberative reflection, at least as far as we can discern from the historical record. It should also be noted that this field of scriptural literature exists within a wider field of other texts—the other texts of antiquity and, indeed, those written since.

The Apocalypse of the Cross

Central to the Christian proclamation was a new way of reading the same scriptures, a change of reading shown graphically by Paul, with his image of Moses being unveiled (2 Cor 4–5): It is an "apocalypse."[13] As Paul puts it:

> Now to him who is able to strengthen you according to my gospel and the preaching of Jesus Christ, according to the apocalypse of the mystery which was kept secret for long ages but is now made manifest and made known through the prophetic writings [κατὰ ἀποκάλυψιν μυστηρίου χρόνοις αἰωνίοις σεσιγημένου φανερωθέντος δὲ νῦν διά τε γραφῶν προφητικῶν . . . γνωρισθέντος], according to the command of the eternal God, to all the nations, to bring about the obedience of faith—to the only wise God be glory for evermore. (Rom 16:25–27)

The mystery hidden from eternity is apocalypsed—that is, unveiled—through the preaching of Jesus Christ, which is now made manifest and known *through the prophetic writings*. Although this passage is often elided in modern critical editions, its point is made elsewhere in Paul, such as his proclamation in 1 Corinthians 15:3–5 that it is of "first importance" that what he received and passes on is that Christ died and rose "in accordance with the scriptures." This is not a particular reference to a particular verse but rather the point that the paschal mystery is to be expounded by drawing upon the full palette of scripture. This is the point made by Barr earlier: Paul was interpreting Christ through the images of the scriptures, using various exegetical methods, no doubt, though the point is not the method but the one being expounding.

Irenaeus gives us the fullest statement regarding this "apocalyptic" reading of scripture, specifying that the unveiling is effected specifically by the cross:

---

13. It should be noted that the term "apocalypse," meaning "unveiling," is connected to but also distinct from other uses of the term, such as to denote a genre, a socio-political movement, or an "invasion from above." In fact, using the term "apocalypse" to refer to a genre seems to be a category mistake: it is first used as a "title" by John, and yet, although his Apocalypse certainly has literary similarities with, say, 1 Enoch, 1 Enoch is not called an "apocalypse" (nor is any other Second Temple text). Classifying texts with similar literary features as "apocalypses," and then explaining John in terms of these other works, overlooks the fact that makes his text highly distinctive: it is written in his own name and in the present. Other uses of the term "apocalypse" (as a social-political movement or an "invasion from above," etc.) are all derivative from this initial transfer of the term.

> If anyone, therefore, reads the Scriptures this way, he will find in them the Word concerning the Christ, and the prefiguration of the new calling. For this one is the "treasure which was hidden in the field" [Matt 13:44], that is, in this world—for "the field is the world" [Matt 13:38]—[a treasure] hidden in the Scriptures, for he was indicated by means of types and parables, which could not be understood by human beings prior to the consummation of those things which had been predicted, that is, the advent of the Lord. And therefore it was said to Daniel the prophet, "Shut up the words, and seal the book, until the time of the consummation, until many learn and knowledge abounds. For, when the dispersion shall be accomplished, they shall know all these things" [Dan 12:4, 7]. And Jeremiah also says, "In the last days they shall understand these things" [Jer 23:20]. For every prophecy, before its fulfillment, is nothing but an enigma and ambiguity to human beings; but when the time has arrived, and the prediction has come to pass, then it has an exact exposition [ἐξήγησις].
>
> And for this reason, when at this present time the Law is read by the Jews, it is like a myth, for they do not possess the explanation [ἐξήγησις] of all things which pertain to the human advent of the Son of God; but when it is read by Christians, it is a treasure, hidden in a field,
> but unveiled [ἀποκαλυπτόμενος] by the cross of the Christ,
> and explained, both enriching the understanding of human beings,
> and showing forth the wisdom of God,
> and making known his economies with regard to the human being,
> and prefiguring the kingdom of the Christ,
> and preaching in anticipation the good news of the inheritance of the holy Jerusalem,
> and proclaiming beforehand that the human being who loves God shall advance so far as even to see God, and hear his Word, and be glorified, from hearing his speech, to such an extent, that others will not be able to behold his glorious countenance [cf. 2 Cor 3:7], as was said by Daniel, "Those who understand shall shine as the brightness of the firmament, and many of the righteous as the stars for ever and ever" [Dan 12:3].
> In this manner, then, I have shown it to be, if anyone read the Scriptures. (*Haer.* 4.26.1)

Unveiled by the cross, the scriptures (OT) have a specific exegesis that enables them to be read not as a "myth" but in terms of "types and parables," and an exegesis that, moreover, illuminates the reader, so they themselves are the ones glorified.

Applying the cross to the field of literature gives us:

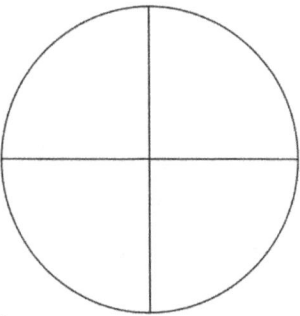

Figure 3

Scripture unveiled by the cross gives a shape to the whole; it is, to use Irenaeus's well-known image, a mosaic of the king: his opponents have disregarded "the order and connection of the Scriptures," transferring the tesserae of the mosaic to produce a picture of a fox (and a bad one at that), thereby dismembering the body of truth (*Haer.* 1.8–9). That diverse texts are thus unified, by the cross, as a body of scripture is something that has also been noted by modern scholars. Richard Hays, for instance, describes how the "eschatological *apokalypsis* of the Cross" inverts Paul's readings of the text so that "when Scripture is refracted through the hermeneutical lens provided by God's action in the crucified Messiah and in forming his eschatological community, it acquires a profound new symbolic coherence."[14] J. Louis Martyn puts it in an even stronger manner: "In a word, with Jesus' glorification, belief in Scripture *comes into being*, by acquiring an indelible link to belief in Jesus' words and deeds."[15] It might perhaps be better to say that these texts are now constituted as (Christian) scripture.

Much work has been done on the literary and rhetorical background of the terms used in Irenaeus's image of scripture as a mosaic, such as "canon," "hypothesis," and "economy."[16] The image of a text as being a living organism of course goes back to the *Phaedrus*, and in Irenaeus's own period Quintilian (*Instit.* 7.10.14–17) describes the words of a speech being arranged as the members of a body. Ps-Longinus, in the work *On the Sublime*, makes a

---

14. Hays, *Echoes of Scripture*, 169.
15. Martyn, "John and Paul," 216, italics original.
16. See Briggman, "Literary and Rhetorical Theory in Irenaeus."

further point which takes us to the relationship between the arrangement of these texts and the proclamation of the gospel and its effect:

> We observe that adeptness in invention and the ordering and economy of subject matter reveal themselves not at separate points but gradually and in the entire fabric of the discourse, whereas sublimity erupts at key moments, rips through the whole subject matter like a lightning bolt, and instantly manifests the speaker's concentrated powers. (*Sublime* 1.4)

Transposing Ps-Longinus to Irenaeus's image of scripture as a mosaic would suggest that seeing the details of the ordering and economy of the scriptures emerges gradually, by perusing the entire scriptures, but seeing the face of the king is like being struck by a lightning bolt, a moment of recognition (cf. Luke 24). In a similar manner, for Clement of Alexandria, it is "the dominical Scripture and voice" that is the true criterion, so if we grasp by faith the indemonstrable first principle, we will be trained "by the voice of the Lord to the knowledge of truth" (*Strom.* 7.16.95.4–6). As Dragoș Andrei Giulea, puts it: "The words of Scripture represent a vehicle of the divine manifestation that is given through the material mediation of the acoustically or visually perceived word."[17] We need to hear the voice of the Lord speaking through the scriptures (OT), for the gospel (singular) is the sublime message of the divine rhetor.

The New Testament as Recapitulation

In this way of looking at scripture, the writings of the apostles and evangelists constitute not "what happened next"—a New Testament following an Old Testament—but the unveiling of the eternal mystery, as Paul put it, hidden in the scripture, brought to light by the cross and proclaimed through the same writings. We can see beautiful examples of such exegetical proclamations in the early Christian literature: Melito of Sardis in his *Peri Pascha* expounds the paschal mystery that is the Christ by unveiling the scriptures, culminating in the risen Christ speaking in the present through Melito himself. Indeed, this exegetical practice and performance is taken by Clement of Alexandria as the very definition of the canon: "The ecclesiastical canon is the concord and symphony of the Law and the prophets in the Parousia of the Lord" (*Strom.* 6.15.125.3).

---

17. Giulea, "Apprehending 'Demonstrations,'" 201–2.

Likewise, Irenaeus, for instance, exhorts Marcion: "Read with earnest care that Gospel which has been conveyed to us by the apostles, and read with earnest care the prophets, and you will find that the whole conduct, and all the doctrine, and all the sufferings of our Lord, were predicted through them" (*Haer.* 4.34.1). Not only did the prophets speak about Christ and his passion, but they did so as a past event: When Isaiah says, "I have seen with my eyes the King, the Lord of hosts," and the other prophets, similarly, in their words, visions, and mode of life, according to Irenaeus, they "see the Son of God as a human being, conversing with human beings, while prophesying what was to happen, saying that he who was not come as yet was present, proclaiming also the impassible as subject to suffering, and declaring that he who was then in heaven had descended [*descendisse*] into the dust of death" (*Haer.* 4.20.8). It is because Christ died on the cross that Isaiah speaks this way, not the other way round.

So, rather than "what happened next," the writings of the apostles and the evangelists are a "recapitulation" of the whole of scripture. Discussions of "recapitulation" often start by turning to Ephesians 1:10, where Paul speaks the mystery of the will of God set forth in Christ, the plan, the "economy," that in the fullness of time all things will be recapitulated in Christ. The background of the term, however, is again a rhetorical one: It is, according to Quintilian, "the repetition and assemblage of facts" which "both refreshes the memory of the judge and places the whole cause before his eyes at once; even if this had not made much impression when the points were made individually, it is cumulatively powerful" (*Instit.* 6.1.1). The only other time Paul uses the word, it is precisely in such a literary manner:

> The commandments, "You shall not commit adultery, You shall not kill, You shall not steal, You shall not covet," and any other commandment, are summed up in this word [ἐν τῷ λόγῳ τούτῳ ἀνακεφαλαιοῦται], "You shall love your neighbor as yourself." (Rom 13:9)

Irenaeus brings this verse together with Isaiah 10:22–23, quoted by Paul a few verses earlier: "He will complete and cut short [his] Word in righteousness, for God will make a concise Word in all the world" (Rom 9:28).[18] The apostolic proclamation of the gospel in accordance with the scriptures is a summary, a concise word, recapitulating the scriptures with greater (the

---

18. λόγον γὰρ συντελῶν καὶ συντέμνων ἐν δικαιοσύνῃ, ὅτι λόγον συντετμημένον ποιήσει ὁ θεὸς ἐν τῇ οἰκουμένῃ ὅλῃ. Most modern translations obscure this.

greatest) force. As such, the proclamation of the gospel, and the writings of the apostles and evangelists, can perhaps be represented as a smaller circle, bringing into focus the larger picture:

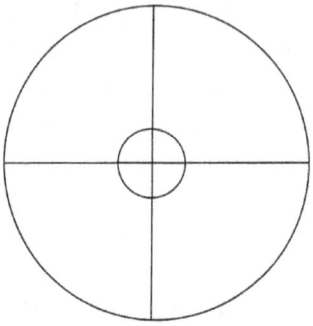

Figure 4

1 Corinthians 15

Having begun the fifteenth chapter of his First Letter to the Corinthians by stating the terms in which he preached the gospel, towards the end of the chapter, Paul then puts in parallel the beginning, the first Adam, and the end, the last Adam, a movement or axis that is both horizontal and vertical: the first is from the earth, the last is from the heavens (vv. 45–48). With the axes of the cross inscribing the scriptures, we are now able to plot the movement from Adam to Christ, tracing the horizontal line of what, since Johannes C. K. von Hofmann, has been called *Heilsgeschichte*, "salvation history," but that figures in the early period spoke of, using another rhetorical term, as the *economy*.[19]

---

19. For a full study of the theology of "salvation history" and its vicissitudes in the twentieth century, see Yarbrough, *Salvation Historical Fallacy*.

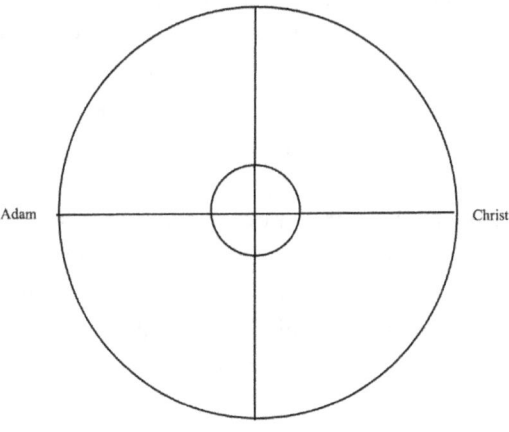

Figure 5

A movement from beginning to end, from Adam to Christ, can indeed be traced, but it is important to note that this plot is told from the point of view of the end, both because we are reading the scriptures, now unveiled, in the light of Christ, and because if Adam is, as Paul puts it in Romans, "the type of the one to come" (5:14), then Christ does indeed come first, in just the same way that a seal precedes its imprint in the wax. This point, with dramatic implications (to be explored later), was maintained in patristic literature from Ignatius and Irenaeus all the way through the first millennium and beyond. For instance, Nicholas Cabasilas, in the fourteenth century, states, quite simply:

> The old [Adam] was not the paradigm for the new, but the new Adam for the old. . . . For, on account of its nature, the old Adam might be the archetype to us, who have known that one first; but to the one before whose eyes are all things before they exist, the older is the imitation of the second, and in accordance with the form and image of that one was the other made, but did not remain so; rather, he was set in motion towards it [the form/image], but did not attain it. . . . To sum it up: the Savior first and alone showed to us the true human, who is perfect on account of both character and life and in all other respects as well. (*Life of Christ* 6.92–94)

This position, of course, resonates with that advocated by Karl Barth: "Man's essential and original nature is to be found, therefore, not in Adam but in Christ. In Adam we can only find it prefigured. Adam can therefore be interpreted only in the light of Christ and not the other way round."[20] Or, again, in words that resemble Cabasilas even closer: "Christ who seems to come second, really comes first, and Adam who seems to come first really comes second."[21] However, the claim made by Wilhelm Pauck in his introduction to Barth's essay is hardly justifiable: "By-passing the entire exegetical and theological tradition built upon this chapter of the Pauline Epistle [Rom 5], Barth offers an entirely new and unprecedented interpretation of the conception of the man implied in the Apostle's view of the relation between Christ and Adam."[22] It would, in fact, seem to be the common interpretation through the first millennium and into the second, perhaps until the advent of the printed Bible and the change of perspective that this opened up (Figure 1).

Barth does differ, however, from the hermeneutical approach we have been tracing and will explore further, by seeing the relationship between type and reality as an invasion: "It is because Christ has thus invaded the world of Adam and claimed it for Himself, that Paul can find a connection between the two, a way that leads from Adam to Christ for himself and all believers."[23] Paul certainly speaks of "the second human" as being "from heaven," in contrast to "the first human" who is "from the earth" (1 Cor 15:47), in a vertical axis, as it were; but before he does that, and before we turn to that dimension, we should note that the prior contrast he gives is horizontal, not vertical: The first human is "psychic" (τὸ ψυχικόν), that is, animated by a breath of life, while the last is "spiritual" (τὸ πνευματικόν, vv. 45–46).

It is important to note that here Paul does not present this as a movement from an initial perfection, followed by "the fall" and the introduction of death, to the regaining of an original or superior perfection. It is rather a movement from the one who comes into being from the earth, animated by a breath, to the one from or of heaven, one who is spiritual and life-giving. It should also be noted that this movement, moreover, transitions through the death and resurrection of Jesus rather than simply contrasting two different points of origin, as Apollinarius took it (and perhaps Barth).[24] This is similarly the case earlier in the same chapter:

---

20. Barth, *Christ and Adam*, 39–40.
21. Barth, *Christ and Adam*, 75.
22. Pauck, "Introduction," to Barth, *Christ and Adam*, 8.
23. Barth, *Christ and Adam*, 61.
24. See Greer, "Man from Heaven".

> For, since by a human death, [then] also by a human resurrection of [the] dead.
> For, just as in the Adam all die, so in the Christ all will be vivified. (1 Cor 15:21–22)[25]

This verse says nothing about sin or a fall; rather, the contrast is between the starting point and end point. In one, the first, we die; in the other, the end, resurrection is granted to the dead. It is a transition from an initial state of animation by a breath, in a mortal state of existence, to vivification through the Spirit. This is exactly how Irenaeus takes it:

> Just as, from the beginning [*ab initio*] of our formation [*plasmationis*] in Adam, the breath of life from God, having been united [*unita*] to the handiwork [*plasmati*], animated [*animavit*] the human being and showed him to be a rational being, so also, at the end [*in fine*], the Word of the Father and the Spirit of God, having become united [*adunitus*] with the ancient substance of the formation [*plasmationis*] of Adam, rendered [*effecit*] the human being living [*viventem*] and perfect, bearing the perfect Father, in order that just as in the animated we all die, so also in the spiritual we may all be vivified [*vivificemur*]. For never at any time did Adam escape the Hands of God, to whom the Father speaking, said, "Let us make the human being in our image, after our likeness" [Gen 1:26]. And for this reason at the end [*fine*], "not by the will of the flesh, nor by the will of man" [John 1:13], but by the good pleasure of the Father, his Hands perfected a living human being [*vivum perfecerunt hominem*], in order that Adam might become in the image and likeness of God. (*Haer.* 5.1.3)

The movement from animation by breath, a formation in which we all die, to the vivification in Christ by the Spirit is such that it is only at the end, as a result of the continuous work of the Hands of God, that Adam finally becomes in the image and likeness of God.

Later in the same book, Irenaeus draws upon verses from Isaiah (42:5; 57:16 LXX) to contrast further the breath and the Spirit: The breath is something created, while the Spirit goes forth from God, so the Spirit is particularly ranked with God, poured out in the last times upon the human race by the adoption of sons. He then continues:

> What has been made is a different thing from him who makes it.
> The breath, then, is temporal, but the Spirit eternal. The breath,

---

25. ἐπειδὴ γὰρ δι' ἀνθρώπου θάνατος, καὶ δι' ἀνθρώπου ἀνάστασις νεκρῶν. ὥσπερ γὰρ ἐν τῷ Ἀδὰμ πάντες ἀποθνήσκουσιν, οὕτως καὶ ἐν τῷ Χριστῷ πάντες ζῳοποιηθήσονται.

too, increases [in strength] for a short period, and continues for a certain time; after that it takes its departure, leaving its former abode destitute of breath. But when the Spirit pervades the human within and without, inasmuch as it continues there, it never leaves him. (*Haer.* 5.12.1–2)

Then turning to Paul, Irenaeus reminds us that it is not the spiritual that is first, with reference to us human beings, but the animated, and only then the spiritual. The economy is, for Irenaeus, the process of God and the human becoming accustomed to each other, the Spirit learning to dwell in human beings, sporadically at first, but perfectly and permanently in Christ, while the human being learns to bear the Spirit of God.[26] The horizontal movement from Adam to Christ is thus movement from type to reality: the first Adam is a type, while perfect or complete humanity is shown in the stature of the fullness of Christ (cf. Eph 4:13), so that, as Irenaeus also has it, Adam is but an infant.[27]

This contrast between breath-animation//Spirit-vivification is of course also one that Christ himself makes, in his words about preserving and losing life, most clearly in the Gospel of Luke (17:33): "Whoever seeks to preserve their animation [ψυχὴν] will lose it; but whoever loses it will make it live [ζωογονήσει αὐτήν]." The background of the word used here, ζωογονήσει, regularly obscured in translations, would seem to be 1 Kgdms (1 Sam) 2:6: "The LORD kills and makes alive [κύριος θανατοῖ καὶ ζωογονεῖ], he leads down to Hades and raises up." It is also implied in other ways, for instance, in Christ's saying, "I have come that you might have life [ζωή]" (John 10:10), the implication being that we don't have "life" apart from in and through Christ.

What, then, of the other contrast mentioned by Paul, the vertical contrast between heaven and earth? Unveiling the scriptures at the end not only enables plotting the horizontal line from Adam to Christ but also opens up another dimension to the narrative. A feature intrinsic to narratives is that once the end has been reached, a perspective is unveiled that was not available to the characters described—or the reader—during the course of the narrative itself (for it would ruin the plot!). A very clear example of this is in the narrative about Joseph in Genesis: although sold into slavery,

---

26. See Irenaeus, *Haer.* 3.17.1; 3.20.2; 4.5.4; 4.14.2; 4.21.3; 4.38.1; 5.3.3; 5.8.1; 5.32.1; 5.35.1; 5.36.3; Évieux, "La Théologie."

27. See Irenaeus, *Dem.* 12–14; *Haer.* 3.22.4; 3.23.5. See also Theophilus of Antioch, *Autol.* 2.25; Clement of Alexandria, *Strom.* 3.14.94; 3.17.102–3. In the fourth century, Ephrem of Syria describes the idea as "pagan" (*Com. Gen.* 14; cf. Steenberg, "Children in Paradise").

sinfully, by his brothers, at the end of this particular narrative arc, Joseph can say: "I am your brother, Joseph, whom you sold into Egypt. And now do not be distressed, or angry with yourselves, because you sold me here; for God sent me before you to preserve life" (Gen 45:4–5). This higher or heavenly dimension of the narrative is hidden from the characters during the unfolding of the plot, to be revealed only at the end, thereby enabling us to see a double narrative—a divine plot being worked out throughout the human plot yet unknown to the humans involved. It is vitally important, however, to note that these two narratives cannot simply be folded into one, at least from the human perspective, without destroying the narrative itself. Similarly, in Peter's speech in Acts:

> This one [Jesus]—delivered up by the determined plan and with the foreknowledge God—you killed, affixing him with nails by the hand of those without the law, him whom God raised up by loosening the birth-pangs of death, because it was not possible for him to be restrained by it. (2:23–24)

What had been done bloodily and lawlessly by humans upon earth is, nevertheless, revealed to be the definite plan from the beginning, with death now becoming a birth (something to which we will return).

With this higher or heavenly dimension now unveiled, the four points of the cross-wise axes (beginning–end, above–below), used by Paul to map out the relation between Adam and Christ in 1 Corinthians 15, can now be plotted more fully:

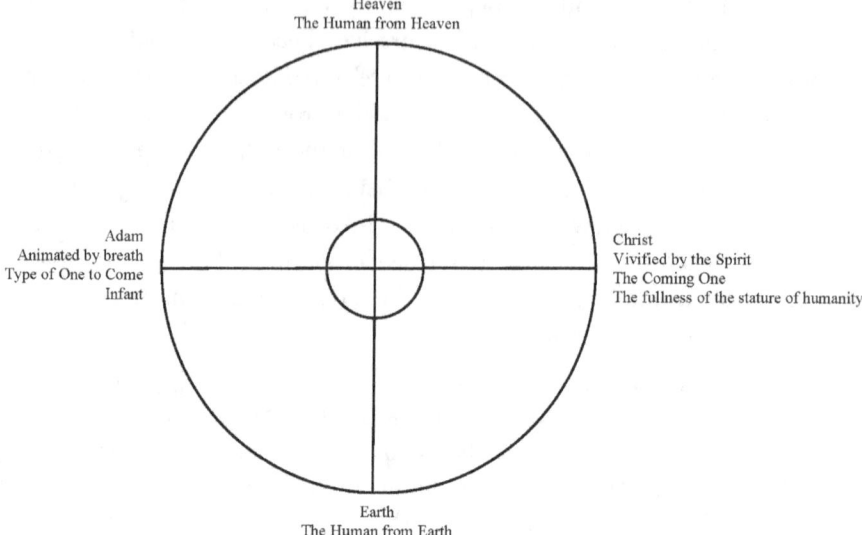

Figure 6

This crosswise dynamic of reading scripture is intrinsic to the way that Paul proclaims the gospel. And, intriguingly, speculation about such correlation is prohibited in the Mishnah: "Whoever gives his mind to four things it were better for him if he had not come into the world: What is above? What is below? What was beforetime? And what will be hereafter?"[28]

That Paul makes a contrast between two forms of life, rather than two "ages," is something that has recently been highlighted by L. Ann Jervis, who argues that this is in fact a contrast between two forms of temporality: "death time" and "life time."[29] Paul, she observes, does not speak of the new age: "Paul regarded not the new age, but life in and with Christ as God's goal for humanity."[30] In further reflecting on the "life-time" opened up in Christ, she makes the further very important point that this "life time"

28. Mishnah, *Hagigah* 2.1 [Danby]. *The Oxford Annotated Mishnah* [Cohen et al.], translates as: "What is upward? What is downward? What is forward? What is backward?," noting: "A formula signifying the intellectual search into all places. The translation 'forward' and 'backwards' keeps all four adverbs as describing space, but some have understood the last two adverbs as describing time, 'beforetime' and 'hereafter.'" On this passage, see also Rowland and Morray-Jones, *Mystery of God*, 221–27.

29. Jervis, *Paul and Time*, 71.

30. Jervis, *Paul and Time*, 49.

embraces all time: "Christ's time envelops human chronological time" so that Christians are already embraced within this.[31]

> Paul does not describe believers as partially in Christ and partially in the present age. They are entirely in Christ. (It may need to be pointed out that union with Christ is not the same as conformity to Christ. Believers become like Christ through an ongoing process that can only take place by recognizing their union [Phil 3:8–11]. That is, Paul does not present union with Christ as incomplete, though conformity to Christ may be [Gal 4:19]). Importantly, it is Christ himself and not the new age that Paul conceives of as God's redemptive goal. Christ dominates the apostle's thinking—a being whose resurrection and exaltation Paul regards as offering a space and a time separate from that of the present evil age.[32]

While Christians, in Christ's life-time, must still await the end, this period of waiting is then, as is every time, encompassed by Christ himself: "Those joined to Christ wait for the future in chronological time, *enveloped by Christ's time*."[33] It is, as we saw earlier, that reading from the end opens up a perspective and horizon that embraces everything from, and including, the beginning.

Jervis describes "Christ time" not as a parallel stretch of chronological time but rather as a quality of life. As she puts it: "Being God, God lives eventful, changeful temporality without the blinkers and boundaries of tenses as humanity experiences tenses."[34] However, while Jervis is certainly correct that Paul does not speak in terms of two ages, neither does he use the language of "time" as she does (death-time and Life-time/Christ's time). It would, I would suggest, be better to use the language of Paul, as we have seen it explored further by Irenaeus, that is, the qualification of the first Adam as animated by breath and the last Adam as a life-giving spirit, with, as we will see, time being the medium through which growth is effected from one state to another, from infancy to maturity.

But before we turn to the question of time, however, we must consider the other passage where Paul connects death to sin, that is Romans 5:12–14:

---

31. Jervis, *Paul and Time*, 107.
32. Jervis, *Paul and Time*, 56–57.
33. Jervis, *Paul and Time*, 125, italics original.
34. Jervis, *Paul and Time*, 69–70.

> Therefore, as sin entered into the cosmos through one human and death through sin, so death spread to all humans because/whereupon all humans sinned;
> for prior to the Law there was sin in the cosmos, but when there is no Law sin is not taken account of, yet nevertheless death reigned from Adam till Moses, even over those who did not commit sin in the likeness of the transgression of Adam, who is a type of the one to come.[35]

These verses are usually taken as referring to a "fall" from immortality to mortality: death entered the world through sin, so death itself, mortality, is something brought about by sin and an enemy to be conquered. But as Jervis notes, "Paul does not think that believers' death is a problem," nor is he "much exercised about the fact that believers currently have mortal bodies."[36]

Similarly, James Barr, as alluded to earlier, has clearly demonstrated that there is no sense in the scriptures (OT) that death was unnatural or that Adam was originally immortal. Barr makes the very important point that we should carefully discern between two different ways in which the word "death" is used in the scriptures, either as the (natural) act of dying or as a poetical or metaphorical force opposing God. The Wisdom of Solomon (1:13) does indeed assert that "God did not create death," a unique statement in the scriptures, but God certainly brings about death: "The LORD kills and makes alive" (1 Kgdms [1 Sam] 2:6). "Certainly Genesis 1 says nothing about God's creation of death," Barr observes, but adds, "Yet perhaps silence about death does not mean that death was not part of the world as created? Darkness was not created, yet darkness was part of the created world."[37] "God is supremely the giver of life," he continues later, "but life does not mean life without limit." Moreover, with a proper burial and with offspring, death is depicted in scripture as both "completion and fulfilment."[38] And this, he comments, is an insight maintained in Christianity:

> When a man or woman grows old and dies peacefully, their families around them, their life's work complete, their faith in God

---

35. Διὰ τοῦτο ὥσπερ δι' ἑνὸς ἀνθρώπου ἡ ἁμαρτία εἰς τὸν κόσμον εἰσῆλθεν καὶ διὰ τῆς ἁμαρτίας ὁ θάνατος, καὶ οὕτως εἰς πάντας ἀνθρώπους ὁ θάνατος διῆλθεν, ἐφ' ᾧ πάντες ἥμαρτον· ἄχρι γὰρ νόμου ἁμαρτία ἦν ἐν κόσμῳ, ἁμαρτία δὲ οὐκ ἐλλογεῖται μὴ ὄντος νόμου, ἀλλ' ἐβασίλευσεν ὁ θάνατος ἀπὸ Ἀδὰμ μέχρι Μωϋσέως καὶ ἐπὶ τοὺς μὴ ἁμαρτήσαντας ἐπὶ τῷ ὁμοιώματι τῆς παραβάσεως Ἀδὰμ ὅς ἐστιν τύπος τοῦ μέλλοντος.
36. Jervis, *Paul and Time*, 105.
37. Barr, *Garden of Eden*, 25.
38. Barr, *Garden of Eden*, 27–28.

calm and untroubled, we do not say in our funeral liturgies that this ending of life manifests the power of sin and its destructive effects. Of course we do not. It is a good death. And in ancient Israel it was so also. Such a death is not "unnatural," it is not "against the will of God," and surely few think so.[39]

Indeed, a peaceful and blessed ending to life is something that Christians have prayed for throughout the centuries. Such death is simply the correlate of coming-into-being (*genesis*): as Irenaeus put it, "all things which have a beginning in time must of course have an end in time also" (*Haer.* 4.4.1).

However, quite distinct from this use of the word "death" (as the natural act of dying), Barr argues, is the poetic use of the word:

> For the discussion of such questions as whether for biblical man death was "natural" or not, we have to observe the existence of a semantic gap between what *we* are meaning and what the biblical language is referring to. For when a biblical poet in sickness or deep trouble thinks that he is being brought into the realm of "death" or "brought down to Sheol," or that weakness of life is a form of death, we have to recognize that "death" in such terms is not the same thing as what we call death.... If we were to apply the biblical usages univocally to our own life, then all the patients in the emergency ward of a hospital would be "dead."... "Death" in this poetic, biblical sense may be a curse, may be opposition to God, may be a force that challenges him and opposes him, but that only proves that we are talking about something other than death.[40]

In this poetic sense, "death" is distinct from and other than the simple bare fact of dying a natural death. One might perhaps capitalize this poetic or metaphorical use of the word: as a force opposing God, it is "Death!"

This observation, I would suggest, enables us to see something odd in the words of Paul in Romans 5:12–14. While it is usually taken as saying that "death" (in our normal usage—the physical and natural act of dying) only began after the first sin (with the implication that there was no death *at all* prior to this), Paul speaks not of death as beginning but as *entering into* the cosmos when sin entered into the cosmos. This is a rather paradoxical turn of phrase, for death, in its usual sense, is a departure from the world. As such, "death" here is best taken not only in the poetic sense identified by Barr, the force opposing God, but also, equally, something other

---

39. Barr, *Garden of Eden*, 27.
40. Barr, *Garden of Eden*, 33–34, italics original.

than "death" in its normal usage. In other words, here Paul is not claiming that mortality as such only began after a primordial sin ruptured an initial immortal perfection (as if no animal or plant ever died before that); such death is rather the correlate of coming-into-being (*genesis*). Rather, death *coming into the world* expresses more the power of death, the hold that it takes in our imagination: Death capitalized.

Moreover, as Paul continues, it is from Adam himself, not after a "fall," that death has reigned, and it has done so even when sin was not taken account of, that is, before Moses and the law. Mortality as such is not the result of an accounting or punishment for sin. The *reign* of death is, thus, not the simple fact of mortality, but more, as Hebrews 2:14–15 puts it, "the *fear* of death" that holds humans in "lifelong *bondage*," subservient not to death as mortality but "to the one who has the power of death, that is, the devil." Similarly, when Paul concludes 1 Corinthians 15 with the quotation from Hosea 13:14, "Where, O death, is your victory? Where, O death, is your sting?," he then comments that "the sting *of death* is sin, and the power of sin is the law" (1 Cor 15:56). It is not death that is a sting of sin, but sin that is the "sting of death," and it is this sin, not mortality, on which Paul focuses. For Paul, the problem is not the natural act of death itself but rather its "sting," sin, which has its power in the law and the awareness of, and accountability for, sin that this awakens.

Double Narrative and Reversal

There is one further feature of reading from the end that must be noted, and that is the reversal that it effects. This is stated most dramatically by Origen, though we can see it reflected upon earlier in Irenaeus and thereafter, up to figures such as Robert Grosseteste.[41] Although Origen is known for allegory and proposing that there are three levels of meaning in scripture, parallel to the human being, when he turns to explaining how scripture is to be understood, it is in terms of a double narrative with a reversal as its turning point (*Princ.* 4.3.4–13). He begins by observing that the scriptures relate how God chose a nation called both Jacob and Israel, divided it into two, then later David built his city Jerusalem, which is the mother-city of Judah, and so on (*Princ.* 4.3.6). But noting how Paul speaks of Israel "according to the flesh" (1 Cor 10:18), implying that there is "an Israel according to the Spirit," similar to the Pauline contrast between "a Jew openly" and "a Jew

---

41. See Irenaeus, *Haer.* 3.22.3–4; Grosseteste, *Cessation of the Laws* 3.2.5.

in secret" (Rom 2:28–29), Origen then continues in an intriguing passage preserved in Greek by Basil and Gregory but left untranslated by Rufinus:

> And, so that we do not linger on the topic of the "Jew who is one in secret" and that of "the inner human being," the Israelite, this being sufficient for those not lacking acumen, we return to our subject and say that Jacob was the father of the twelve patriarchs, and they of the rulers of the people, and these again of the rest of the Israelites. So, then, the bodily Israelites have reference to the rulers of the people, and the rulers of the people to the patriarchs, and the patriarchs to Jacob and those still higher up; the spiritual Israelites, on the other hand, of whom the bodily were a type, are they not from the clans, the clans having come from the tribes, and the tribes from some one individual having a *genesis* not of a bodily kind but of the better kind, he too being born from Isaac, and he being descended from Abraham, all referring back up to Adam, whom the Apostle says is Christ? For the beginning of every lineage as [referring] to the God of all began lower down from Christ, who is next to the God and Father of all, being thus the father of every soul, as Adam is the father of all human beings. And if Eve is touched on by Paul as referring to the Church, it is not surprising—Cain being born of Eve and all after him having reference to Eve—to have here types of the Church, they all being born from the Church in a preeminent sense. (*Princ.* 4.3.7)

That is, he contrasts the descending bodily lineage proceeding onwards by bodily birth ("Jacob being the father of the twelve patriarchs," and so on thereafter) with a lineage that proceeds in reverse, through "a *genesis* not of a bodily kind but of the better kind," which results in a lineage that returns all the way "back up to Adam, whom the Apostle says is Christ." Origen probably has in mind the difference between the genealogy given in Matthew, where "the *genesis* of Jesus" (Matt 1:1, 18) is described as a line descending from Abraham (not Adam), and that of Luke (3:28–38), which traces the lineage backwards or upwards to Adam, the son of God: The first lineage traces the bodily descent according to the flesh, back to Jacob and those before him, arriving at its end in Christ, while the second lineage, beginning with Christ, traces the descent, or rather, ascent of the spiritual Israel all the way back to Adam. Moreover, as he puts it: "If Eve is touched on by Paul as referring to the Church" then it is by "all being born from the Church in a preeminent sense" that the lineage ascends back to the beginning, prior to Jacob (or Abraham), the beginning that is Adam, the son of God. What Origen seems to be saying here is that while the human race has continued through sexual procreation and bodily *genesis*, when it arrives at its end, in Christ, a "better kind" of *genesis* comes about, which then proceeds backwards (or upwards), all the way to the origin that is Adam. The first Adam is thus the father of all human beings, while the last Adam, that is Christ, is the father of all those begotten in him.

Before Origen, Irenaeus had also pointed to a "reversal" or "recycling" movement by connecting the genealogy in Luke with Paul's words in Romans 5 and 1 Corinthians 15:

> Wherefore Luke points out that the pedigree which traces the generation of our Lord back to Adam contains seventy-two generations, connecting the end with the beginning, and implying that it is he who has summed up in himself all nations dispersed from Adam downwards, and all languages and generations of humans, together with Adam himself. Hence also was Adam himself termed by Paul "the type of the one to come" [Rom 5:14], because the Word, the Fashioner of all things, prefigured in him the future economy relating to the Son of God on behalf of the human race, God having predetermined the first, the animated human that is, so that he should be saved by the spiritual [one]; for, since the Savior pre-exists, it was necessary that the one to be saved should also exist, so that the Savior should not be without purpose. (*Haer.* 3.22.3)

He then continues by describing a similar "back-referencing" from Mary to Eve, concluding:

> For this reason did the Lord declare that the first should in truth be last, and the last first. And the prophet, too, indicates the same, saying, "instead of fathers, children have been born unto you" [Ps 45:16/44:17]. For the Lord, having been born "the firstborn of the dead" [Col 1:18, *primogenitus enim mortuorum natus Dominus*], and receiving into his bosom the ancient fathers, has regenerated them into the life of God, he having been made himself the beginning of those that live, as Adam became the beginning of those who die. Therefore Luke, commencing the genealogy with the Lord, carried it back to Adam, indicating that it was he who regenerated them into the Gospel of life, and not they him. And thus also it was that the knot of Eve's disobedience was loosed by the obedience of Mary. For what the virgin Eve had bound fast through unbelief, this did the virgin Mary set free through faith. (*Haer* 3.22.4)

The lineage from Adam onwards is that of mortal beings; whereas the genealogy that returns from the Lord back to Adam is that of life, so the Lord has been born "the firstborn of the dead." We will explore this "birth" (*gennēsis*), contrasted with "coming-into-being" (*genesis*), further in the next chapter.

The Time of Scripture

What then of (chronological) time and growth? Having "refigured" scripture, we should take one further step, to factor ourselves into the figure, in our act of reading scripture, which is always, and necessarily, done in the present.

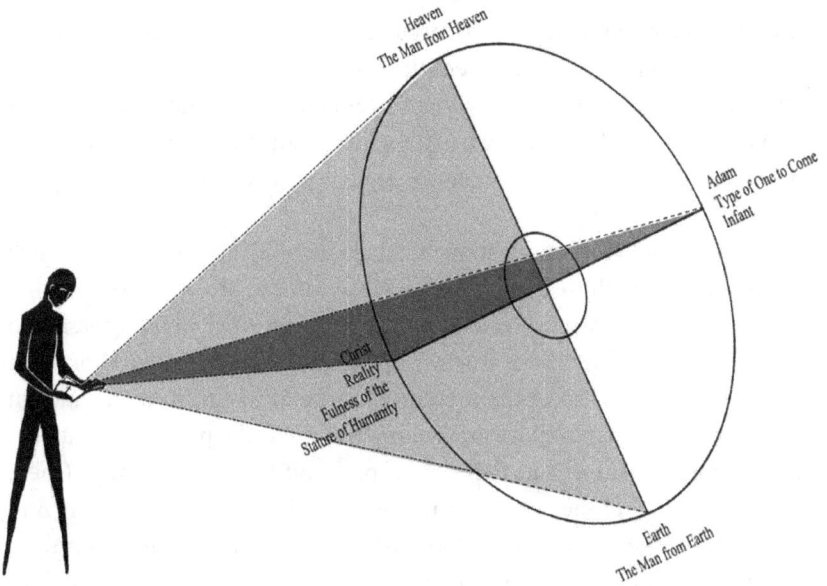

Figure 7

What this image aims to capture is that while reading these texts as Christian scripture, in the way we have unfolded, we, nevertheless, always stand in the present, our own present, with the scriptures being ever more unveiled in the light of the cross (we are at the apex of the cone in the figure, the foot of the cross, indicated by the panes) as *we* move towards our own end, an end—death—that is coterminous, but not synchronous, with Jesus Christ's own end and the end of everything that has come into being. The "time" of scripture, *as scripture*, is thus the time it takes us to read, time during which we grow along the axes we have mapped out. In terms of the "reversal" just considered, one might put it this way: Each one of us has come into being as a result of our parents' act of sexual procreation; in our *genesis* we were passive, with no choice (how could it be otherwise?), coming into being animated by a mortal breath. And so, in terms of this point of origin, it seems to us that the cause of our existence is our biological parents, as it indeed is. However, as we approach our end, our death and resurrection in Christ, we find that the originating cause of our existence is in fact God, our Father, who has chosen us in Christ "before the foundation of the world" (Eph 1:4): our true beginning is only attained at the end. The final cause is, indeed, the originating cause. But through the paschal mystery, which we will explore in the next chapter, the end to which that God has called us from the beginning turns out to be birth (*gennēsis*) into life by the resurrection. In this way, then, the scriptural movement from the first Adam to the last Adam is the same movement for each human being, for humanity as a whole, and, as we will see in the fourth chapter, for Gregory of Nyssa it is the movement of nature itself, as it takes steps from the lower forms of life to the higher.

What more can we say about time, as being the dimension in which we are and in which we grow? We are always in the present: From the beginning, we are thrown down, as it were, between the tick of our *genesis* and the tock of death. Even if we are reading scripture as a narrative about past events, we are doing so in the present; likewise, if we are studying ancient ways of reading scripture, we are again doing so in the present. As Augustine famously pointed out, there *is* no past and there *is* no future (there *was* and *will be*, but they *are* not); all there *is* is the past-in-the-present and the future-in-the-present, and, moreover, this present moment is always passing away (*Conf.* 11.17–28). Each moment is, thus, the last moment of time, a reality we "veil" by projecting a line of time stretching backwards and forwards, relegating Christ's coming to the historical past and to an unspecified future event (Figure 1). If instead we recognize that we are, in the present, reading scripture unveiled by the cross at the end—the end of scripture, of the work of Jesus Chris, and our own end (Figure 7)—then we can take Paul's words seriously: It is "at the fullness of time," the end of time, that Christ has redeemed us, effecting our adoption (Gal 4:4). We, however, are still growing to this fullness of time and humanity in Christ (cf. Eph 4:13), a growth that takes place through the temporal movement from the first Adam to the last Adam, from animation to vivification, in the terms of Paul and Irenaeus. As such, time is, as Augustine put it, "the extension of the soul" (*Conf.* 11.33) or, as Plotinus put it: "Time is the life of the soul in its changing motion from one way of living to another" (*Enn.* 3.7.11, 43).

Finally, returning to the sublimity of the gospel, the lightning bolt of the divine rhetor illuminating the whole, we can now see that the gospel is not simply a report of a past event. In the first full analysis of the term "gospel" by a Christian writer, Origen concludes that the term refers generally to those texts "which present the sojourn [ἐπιδημίαν] of Christ and prepare for his coming [παρουσίαν] and produce it [ἐμποιοῦντά τε αὐτὴν] in the souls of those who are willing to receive the Word of God who stands at the door and knocks and wishes to enter their souls" (*Comm. John* 1.26; cf. Rev 3:20). According to "the letter" (i.e., the plain, sense-perceptible meaning of the Gospels), the Gospels narrate a past event; to become *gospel*, according to Origen, that is, an exhortation effecting the coming (the *parousia*) of Christ in the present, they must be "translated" (*Comm. John* 1.45). That is, to put it in a more familiar idiom, without a homily, the reading remains a narrative of the past; the gospel will not have been preached even if a pericope from one of the Gospels has been read.[42] In this way Origen can account for how Christ came spiritually, even before coming bodily, to those who were perfect, those no longer under a pedagogue, that is, those who had already arrived at "the fullness of time," such as the patriarchs, Moses, and the prophets—all those "who contemplated the glory of Christ" (*Comm. John* 1.37; cf. Gal 3:25; 4:4). In reverse, as Origen continues, this also means that "just as Christ visited the perfect before his sojourn which was visible and bodily, so also he has not yet visited those who are still infants after his proclaimed coming [*parousia*], since they are 'under tutors and governors' and have not yet arrived at 'the fullness of the time,'" still needing "the preparation which must take place in those who are about to receive his divinity" (*Comm. John* 1.38; cf. Gal 4:2, 4). In the same way, then, as the law contains "a shadow of the good things to come" (Heb 10:1), Origen concludes that "so also the gospel, which is thought to be understood by all who read it, teaches a shadow of the mysteries of Christ" (*Comm. John* 1.39). It is to these mysteries that we will turn in the next chapter.

42. See Schmemann, *Eucharist*, 77: "For the genuine sermon is neither simply an explanation of what was read by knowledgeable and competent persons, nor a transmission to the listeners of the theological knowledge of the preacher, nor a meditation 'a propos' of the gospel text. In general, it is not a sermon *about the gospel* ('on a gospel theme'), but the preaching of the gospel itself."

2

The Paschal Christ

REFIGURING HOW WE THINK about scripture, as described in the previous chapter, has implications for how we think of Christian theology more generally. If we think within the linear horizon of the implied narrative of "The Bible" (Figure 1), the Old Testament is followed by a series of distinct events: the birth of Jesus Christ at (or as) the incarnation; followed thirty-three years later by the crucifixion; then, three days later, the resurrection; after forty days, the ascension; and then, after a further ten days, Pentecost; followed by the activities and letter-writing of the apostles (and Revelation concluding the book). Our tendency to assume, unreflectively, that these are indeed discrete and distinct events is underwritten not only by our familiarity with "The Bible" but also by having inherited a liturgical calendar in which these are celebrated as distinct feasts on different days. Unreflectively, because we have inherited both "The Bible" and the liturgical calendar as starting points for our theological reflection, ignoring the ways in which these developed, for, of course, the early centuries did not have the former and only an incipient form of the latter.

What, then, would be the shape of Christian theology if we began not with the implied narrative of "The Bible" but the historical, hermeneutical, and liturgical order of scripture (OT) unveiled in the light of the cross, resulting in the proclamation of the gospel, the letters of Paul, and then the Gospels, these texts providing a recapitulation of what was previously hidden in the scriptures now proclaimed through the same scriptures?

The Grammar of Christology

We should begin, of course, with the person of Jesus Christ, the Anointed One, and the doctrine of "the incarnation." According to the *Oxford Dictionary of the Christian Church*, "The Christian doctrine of the incarnation affirms that the eternal Son of God took flesh from his human mother and that the historical Christ is at once both fully God and fully man," a doctrine that "took classical shape under the influence of the controversies of the fourth–fifth centuries."[1] However, as Ingolf Dalferth points out in his fascinating and provocative book *Crucified and Resurrected: Restructuring the Grammar of Christology*, since the nineteenth century, the term has come to stand for Christianity itself: Christianity is, as the subtitle to Charles Gore's influential collection of studies, *Lux Mundi*, put it, "the Religion of the Incarnation."[2] So much is this the case that, as John Hick stated in the preface to the publication of *The Myth of God Incarnate*, "The traditional doctrine of the incarnation has long been something of a shibboleth, exempt from reasoned scrutiny and treated with unquestioning literalness."[3] As the absolute center for Christian theology, as Dalferth puts it,

> the doctrine of the incarnation, as the most concentrated expression of the gospel, holds the dominant theological position among the articles of Christology. In that God's Son, the Second Person of the Trinity, entered our human existence, God took on himself the human condition in such a way that we humans are now in touch with God through the human nature of Jesus Christ. It is therefore not the cross and resurrection but the fact that Christ became human that is the decisive soteriological message of the Christian faith.[4]

Behind this doctrine lies, of course, the affirmation that "Jesus is the Son of God." But how should the word "is" be understood? Dalferth, in response to Hick, points out that taking the "is" as either indicating class membership, or as giving a definition, or as identification, is problematic, and so settles upon the fourth possibility, that it should be understood as predication.[5]

---

1. Louth, *Oxford Dictionary*, s.v. "incarnation."
2. Dalferth, *Crucified and Risen*, 1–7; Gore, *Lux Mundi*.
3. Hick, *Myth of God Incarnate*, xi, cited by Dalferth, *Crucified and Risen*, 3 (mistakenly given as ix).
4. Dalferth, *Crucified and Risen*, 3–4.
5. Dalferth, *Crucified and Risen*, 13–19, drawing upon Hick, "Christ and Incarnation," 154.

In Accordance with the Scriptures

But here we now enter into a quandary: In the confession that "Jesus is the Son of God," which is the subject and which the predicate? If "Jesus" is the subject of predication, then he is the one being said to be the Son of God, and this then demands a historical assessment of whether Jesus of Nazareth actually demonstrated and possessed all the divine attributes (resulting, as Dalferth points out, in the intense research into the life of Jesus carried out since the nineteenth century and the revival of kenotic Christologies in Lutheran and Anglican theology). If, on the other hand, we take the confession the other way round, then, as Dalferth puts it, "it is not Jesus but the Son of God (i.e., 'Son of God' according to the understanding of the term in classical incarnational Christology), the Logos, the Second Person of the Trinity, who is the subject and of whom it is said that he is Jesus of Nazareth."[6] In this case, he continues, "this analysis imposes, as it were, another subject on the life story of Jesus of Nazareth, with the result that this life story becomes the predicate of a divine person."[7] And herein resides the disquiet that many have had with what is described as "the classic doctrine of the incarnation":

> Even the orthodox solution, as presented to us in the doctrine of an- and en-hypostasia, leaves open the question of whether the full individual humanity of Jesus remains assured. For if what constitutes the person of Jesus is the Logos, the Second Person of the Trinity, so that Jesus is not a self-individuating human subject, then it is not surprising that "Christologies designed around the theme of incarnation have never ever led to the historical and concrete humanity of Jesus of Nazareth."[8]

---

6. Dalferth, *Crucified and Risen*, 18–19.

7. Dalferth, *Crucified and Risen*, 19.

8. Dalferth, *Crucified and Risen*, 19, quoting Pannenberg, "Christologie und Theologie," 134. Earlier, Dalferth asserted: "Every attempt to demonstrate its consistency, such as the Cappadocians' doctrine of an- and en-hypostasia and its assimilation into modern (Protestant) theology; assumptus, habitus, and subsistence theories of Scholastic theologies; or the kenosis theories of Lutheran and Anglican origin, has called into question either the humanity or the divinity or the unity of the person of Jesus Christ" (8). The Cappadocians, of course, had no such doctrine; it is clearly Dalferth who is reading the assumptions of "modern (Protestant) theology" back into the Cappadocians (cf. Shults, "Dubious Christological Formula"; Gockel, "Dubious Christological Formula?"). It should be noted that my engagement with Dalferth concerns not his analysis of the term anhypostasia/enhypostasia, or indeed the way in which such terminology was refined after Chalcedon, but rather with the question of who the subject of christological reflection actually is.

The Paschal Christ

In other words, when analyzing the confession that "Jesus is the Son of God" in terms of predication, depending on which part of the confession we take to be the subject and which the predicate, we end up with either a Christology from below or from above, and both are unsatisfactory.

The problem here is bound up with the implied narrative of "The Bible" (Figure 1) in which the "incarnation" is understood as a discrete event, the turning point between the Old and New Testament. Dalferth's "restructuring" of the christological grammar, however, points in a similar direction to the refiguring of scripture that we undertook in the previous chapter. Dalferth rightly highlights that the significance of any christological confession is primarily soteriological, and adds that "the only reason these confessions have soteriological significance is that they do not speak merely of Jesus of Nazareth; they speak of the *Jesus Christ who was raised from the dead by God.*"[9] Salvation, Dalferth further argues,

> does not stem primarily from *what* the Christological confessions declare concerning Jesus; it stems from the fact that they declare it *concerning him*. Christians confess Jesus as Son of God, Lord, Savior, Word of God, and so on, for this reason: they know him to be *the one who was crucified and whom God raised from the dead*.[10]

As such, he argues, if we want to understand the logical structure of christological confessions coherently, "their content must always be reconstrued as a statement *concerning the one who has been crucified and raised*. In other words, it is not the tangible historical Jesus in isolation who is the point of reference, and thus the topic, of Christological confessions, but Jesus Christ raised from the dead by God."[11] This is an inescapable fact for Dalferth, and it holds for all confessions and creedal statements as well as all narrative and discursive texts in the New Testament, including the Gospels, which are, in his words, "no more and no less than interpretations of the resurrection message as proclaimed in the events of Jesus's life."[12]

Finally, this underlying paschal dimension of each and every christological confession, from the beginning, enables Dalferth to hint towards a nuanced distinction between the way we speak about Jesus and Jesus Christ in such a way that incorporates how we speak about God and about ourselves:

9. Dalferth, *Crucified and Risen*, 21, italics original.
10. Dalferth, *Crucified and Risen*, 24, italics original.
11. Dalferth, *Crucified and Risen*, 24, italics original.
12. Dalferth, *Crucified and Risen*, 24.

> Right from the outset, therefore, the Christian faith has never doubted that the one who has been raised is *the crucified Jesus of Nazareth* (resurrection of *Jesus*) and that to speak of his having been raised by God is to acknowledge the occurrence of *an eschatological event that affects not only him but God himself and each one of us* (resurrection of Jesus *Christ*).[13]

It is as crucified and risen that Jesus of Nazareth is Jesus Christ. And so, "the real subject matter of Christology," Dalferth concludes, is not "the historical, tangible Jesus of Nazareth and his exemplary and religious significance for us," but rather "God's *firstborn raised from the dead*."[14]

Rather than continuing with Dalferth's own development of these themes in the remainder of his book, it is worthwhile turning to what is widely acknowledged—and certainly by Dalferth—to be the classic statement on the theme from the fourth century, Athanasius's treatise usually referred to simply as *On the Incarnation*,[15] for not only does it *not* present the subject matter in the manner that is usually assumed to be the "classical shape of the doctrine of the incarnation," but in fact it resonates profoundly with the argument of Dalferth, and in fact even enables us to explicate the subject matter in a more pointed and expansive manner. As Khaled Anatolios has pointed out, *On the Incarnation* and its "first part," *Against the Gentiles*, "are first and foremost an *apologia crucis*."[16] Athanasius begins *Against the Gentiles* by noting that although "the sacred and divinely inspired Scriptures are sufficient for the exposition of the truth," and there are also "many treatises of our blessed teachers" that show how to interpret the scriptures, as these works are not to hand, the task now is to expound what he has learnt from them:

> I mean the faith in Christ the Savior, that no one may regard the teaching of our doctrine [λόγου] as worthless or suppose faith in Christ to be irrational [ἄλογον]. Such things the pagans misrepresent and scorn, greatly mocking us, though they have nothing

---

13. Dalferth, *Crucified and Risen*, 24–25, italics original.

14. Dalferth, *Crucified and Risen*, 31, italics original.

15. The full title of the work is *On the Inhumanization of the Word and His Manifestation to Us Through the Body* (Περὶ τῆς ἐνανθρωπήσεως τοῦ Λόγου καὶ τῆς διὰ σώματος πρὸς ἡμᾶς ἐπιφανείας αὐτοῦ). I will leave for another occasion a full exploration of the different shades of meaning of the words ἐνανθρώπησις ("inhumanization"), ἐνσάρκωσις ("incarnation"), and ἐνσωμάτωσις ("embodiment") and just use the customary word "incarnation" for now.

16. Anatolios, *Athanasius*, 28.

other than the cross of Christ to cite in objection. It is particularly in this respect that one must pity their insensitivity, because in slandering the cross they do not see that its power has filled the whole world, and that through it the effects of the knowledge of God have been revealed to all. For if they had really applied their minds to his divinity they would not have mocked at so great a thing, but would rather have recognized that he was the Savior of the universe and that the cross was not the ruin but the healing of creation. For if, after the cross, all idolatry has been overthrown, and all demonic activity is put to flight by this sign, and Christ alone is worshipped, and through him the Father is known, and opponents are put to shame while he every day invisibly converts their souls—how then, one might reasonably ask them, is this matter still to be considered in human terms, and should one not rather confess that he who ascended the cross is the Word of God and the Savior of the universe? [ὁμολογεῖν Θεοῦ Λόγου καὶ Σωτῆρα εἶναι τοῦ παντὸς τὸν ἐπὶ τοῦ σταυροῦ ἀναβάντα] (*Gent.* 1)

The order of identification is important and consistently rendered thus by Athanasius: it is the one who ascended the cross that is the Word of God and Savior, a point that we have seen made by Dalferth, though in Dalferth's case it is expanded to include the resurrection ("the one who was crucified and whom God raised from the dead" is the subject of Christology, something to which we will return).

Athanasius opens the second part of this work by recapitulating what he had done in the first part and then specifying his present task:

> Let us, with the faith of our religion, relate also the things concerning the incarnation of the Word and expound his divine manifestation to us, which the Jews slander and the Greeks mock, but we ourselves venerate, so that, all the more from his apparent degradation, you may have an even greater and fuller piety towards him, for the more he is mocked by unbelievers by so much he provides a greater witness of his divinity, because what human beings cannot understand as impossible, these he shows to be possible [cf. Matt 19:26], and what human beings mock as unseemly, these he renders fitting by his own goodness, and what human beings through sophistry laugh at as merely human, these by his power he shows to be divine, overturning the illusion of idols by his own apparent degradation through the cross, invisibly persuading those who mock and disbelieve to recognize his divinity and his power. (*Inc.* 1)

The specification that these things are slandered by the Jews and mocked by the Greeks, a clear allusion to 1 Corinthians 1:23, means that the "apparent degradation" is not that of a divine person kenotically assuming a human condition but rather, as he puts it, the "apparent degradation through the cross"—"apparent" because, although foolish and weak by worldly standards, this is in fact the power and wisdom of God, by which he "invisibly persuades" those who mock and disbelieve to recognize his divinity—here, on the cross. As is already clear, the stated aim of the classic text on the incarnation has little to do with what is assumed to be the classic shape of the doctrine of the incarnation but in fact is already focused on that towards which Dalferth aims to reorient christological reflection.

This becomes indisputably clear when we turn to the content of the treatise itself. After the introduction, Athanasius presents two analyses of the "rationality" of the cross and its Word, the first (*Inc.* 2–10) focused upon the dilemma in which the being created by God for life now dies, and the second (*Inc.* 11–19), the dilemma in which the being created by God for knowledge of himself is now ignorant of his maker: What should God do with respect to both these problems? It should be noted that the phrasing of these dilemmas is rhetorical, leading into an analysis of what God has in fact done. The wording of Athanasius's first account of the rationality of the cross is particularly rich and subtle. He speaks of how the Word, having mercy upon the human race, having pity on our weakness, condescending to our corruption, not enduring the dominion of death, lest what had been created should perish and the work of the Father be in vain, "takes for himself a body and that not foreign to our own" (*Inc.* 8). He then continues:

> He takes that which is ours, and that not simply, but from a spotless and stainless virgin, ignorant of man, [a body] pure and unmixed from intercourse with men. Although being himself powerful and the creator of the universe, he prepares for himself in the Virgin the body as a temple, and made it his own, as an instrument, making himself known and dwelling in it. And thus, taking from ours that which is like, since all were liable to the corruption of death, delivering it over to death on behalf of all, he offered it to the Father, doing this in his love for human beings, so that, on the one hand, with all dying in him [πάντων ἀποθανόντων ἐν αὐτῷ] the law concerning corruption in human beings might be undone (its power being fully expended in the lordly body [ἐν τῷ κυριακῷ σώματι] and no longer having any ground against similar human beings), and, on the other hand, that as human beings had turned

towards corruption he might turn them again to incorruptibility and give them life from death, by making the body his own and by the grace of the resurrection banishing death from them as straw from the fire.

For the Word, realizing that in no other way would the corruption of human beings be undone except, simply, by dying, yet being immortal and the Son of the Father the Word was not able to die, for this reason he takes to himself a body capable of death, in order that it, participating in the Word who is above all, might be sufficient for death on behalf of all, and through the indwelling Word would remain incorruptible, and so corruption might henceforth cease from all by the grace of the resurrection. Whence, by offering to death the body he had taken to himself, as an offering holy and free of all spot, he immediately abolished death from all like him, by the offering of a like. For being above all, the Word of God consequently, by offering his own temple and his bodily instrument as a substitute for all, fulfilled in death that which was required; and, being with all through the like [body], the incorruptible Son of God consequently clothed all with incorruptibility in the promise concerning the resurrection. And now the very corruption of death no longer holds ground against human beings because of the Word indwelling in them through the one body [διὰ τὸν ἐνοικήσαντα Λόγον ἐν τούτοις διὰ τοῦ ἑνὸς σώματος]. (*Inc.* 8–9)

When Athanasius speaks of the body that the Word takes from the Virgin, or the body as the temple that he prepares for himself in the Virgin, in which he might dwell and make himself known, the body that he offers to death so that with all dying in him, the law of death and corruption might be loosed, and the body as that which he makes his own by giving others life from death through the grace of the resurrection, and, above all, all this happening "because of the Word indwelling in them through the one body"—all in the present tense—it is clear that Athanasius is not describing here how Jesus was born from his human mother; indeed, he never mentions the name "Mary" in this work. Rather, his analysis of the rationality of the cross speaks of the life-giving death on the cross and the corporate mystery in which this is effected, involving the whole human race.

Athanasius concludes this section by saying: "This, therefore, is the first cause of the incarnation of the Savior. One might also recognize that his gracious advent consistently occurred from the following" (*Inc.* 10). The following, second analysis of the rationality of the cross is developed through the dilemma regarding knowledge and ignorance: having been created to know God through his Word, human beings turned rather to things of sense perception, and so "the Word himself submitted to appear through a body, so that as a human he might bring humans to himself and return their sense perception to himself, and then, seeing him as a human being, he might, through the works he effects, persuade them that he is not human only but God and the Word and Wisdom of the true God" (*Inc.* 16). This persuasion culminates in the cross, for while the disciples continually misunderstood, what is most wonderful, Athanasius says, is that

> even at his death, or rather at the very trophy over death, I mean the cross, all creation confessed that he who was made known and suffered in the body was not simply a human being but Son of God and Savior of all. For the sun turned back and the earth shook and the mountains were rent, and all were awed. These things showed the Christ on the cross to be God [Ταῦτα δὲ τὸν μὲν ἐν τῷ σταυρῷ Χριστὸν Θεὸν ἐδείκνυον] and the whole of creation to be his servant, witnessing in fear the advent [παρουσίαν] of the Master. In this way, then, the God Word showed himself to human beings by his works. (*Inc.* 19)

Athanasius again maintains his consistency in the order of identification: It is the Christ on the cross who is shown to be God, and it is in this way that the God Word reveals himself to human beings by his works.

In what we have seen so far, it is clear that there is indeed a great deal of alignment between Athanasius's treatise and Dalferth's constructive proposal for "restructuring the grammar of Christology" by taking seriously that the one confessed to be the Son of God, Word, Lord, and Savior is always already the one who was crucified and raised from the dead by God. Yet there is also a difference. While Dalferth emphasizes that it is the crucified *and risen* Jesus who is the subject of christological statements, Athanasius instead simply identifies the subject as the one on the cross: "He who ascended the cross is the Word and Savior of the universe" (*Gent.* 1), and the whole of creation witnesses that "the Christ on the cross is God," shaking with fear at his *parousia* there (*Inc.* 19).

In the following chapters, Athanasius focuses his attention on the form of Christ's death, "because this is the chief point of our faith and absolutely all human beings discuss it, so that you may know that also from this, the more rather than the less, Christ is known to be God and the Son of God" (*Inc.* 19). After playing with his readers, by speculating about whether Christ might have died, for instance, from old age or why he had not died a more glorious death, in human terms, only to dismiss such speculations as being "for outsiders" (*Inc.* 25), Athanasius gives various scriptural reasons for the cross (such as "becoming a curse," Gal 3:13; Deut 21:23) and then turns his attention to the resurrection of the body. Strikingly, however, he does not here turn to the Gospel reports of seeing the risen Christ, nor Paul's words about this, but instead focuses all his attention on Christians in the present. By taking up the faith of the cross *they* are the ones who witness to the reality of the resurrection:

> That death has been dissolved, and the cross has become victory over it, and it is no longer strong but is itself truly dead, no mean proof but an evident surety is that it is despised by all Christ's disciples, and everyone tramples on it, and no longer fears it, but with the sign of the cross and faith in Christ tread it under foot as something dead. Of old, before the divine sojourn [ἐπιδημίαν] of the Savior, all used to weep for those dying as if they were perishing. But since the Savior's raising the body, no longer is death fearsome, but all believers in Christ tread on it as nothing, and would rather choose to die than deny their faith in Christ. (*Inc.* 27)

Athanasius concludes this central section of his treatise by emphasizing that, with the witness of Christians now taking up the cross and with even the demons bearing witness to Christ, it should be clear that "the Savior raised up his own body, and that he is the true Son of God, being from him as the Father's own Word and Wisdom and Power, who in the last time took a body for the salvation of all, and taught the world about the Father, destroyed death, granted incorruptibility to all through the promise of the resurrection, raising his own body as the first-fruits and showing it as a trophy over death and its corruption by the sign of the cross" (*Inc.* 32).[17] Athanasius's treatment of the resurrection takes us back to his analysis of the first dilemma and "the one body" spoken of there: the resurrection is not only that of the body of Jesus of Nazareth but "the lordly body" (τοῦ κυριακοῦ σώματος, *Inc.* 31; cf. 8). In Dalferth's terms, it is not simply the "resurrection of *Jesus*" but the "resurrection of Jesus *Christ*." Or, as Origen had put it before Athanasius: "The Resurrection of Christ, which followed

---

17. The treatise continues with a refutation of the Jews and of the gentiles, followed by a short conclusion; it is in the refutation of the gentiles that Athanasius writes "he was incarnate that we might be divinized" (*Inc.* 54), which is usually taken as the central (or even sole) theme of the work, with the presumption that by "incarnation" Athanasius means what we today take as the "classical shape" of the doctrine.

on from his Passion on the Cross, also contains the mystery of the Resurrection of the whole body of Christ" (*Comm. John* 10.229).

From Tomb to Womb

Athanasius's treatment of his subject matter in *On the Incarnation* is clearly as different to what passes as "the classical doctrine of the incarnation" (despite it being continuously referred to as the classical exposition of this doctrine) as is Dalferth's restructured grammar for confessing the crucified and risen one, in ways that are both similar and slightly different. While Dalferth wants to make sure that incarnational language is grounded in a prior confession about the crucified and risen one, Athanasius wants to demonstrate that "he who ascended the cross is the Word of God and Savior of the universe." It is as if, for Athanasius, the incarnation, the cross, and the resurrection have apparently not yet been separated into different "events." To understand how this is so, we should recall the point made by the liturgist Thomas Talley, that the initial expansion of the original single-night Quartodeciman celebration of Pascha on Nisan 14 into a triduum by the end of the second century "contained the seeds that would eventually yield the refraction of the single mystery of redemption into a series of commemorations of discrete historical moments in that mystery."[18] We can see the result of this refraction already in the fourth century in Egeria's account of the liturgical celebrations in Jerusalem, by which time the Paschal celebration had refracted into a full Holy Week and more.[19]

But that this refraction is not a separation into discrete events is made visually, and strikingly, clear in the iconography for the feasts that subsequently developed. The earliest depictions show the living Christ on the cross, as seen in the fifth-century doors of St. Sabina in Rome and the ivory crucifixion in the British Museum as well as, from the sixth century, the Rabbula Gospels and the Lateran reliquary box (see Images 1–4).

---

18. Talley, *Origins of the Liturgical Year*, 39.
19. See Wilkinson, *Egeria's Travels to the Holy Land*.

The Paschal Christ

Image 1: The Crucifixion, panel from the doors of St. Sabina, Rome, 430–432 CE

Image 2: The Crucifixion, panel from an ivory casket, British Museum, 420–430 CE

Image 3: The Crucifixion, Rabbula Gospels, Syria, sixth century

Image 4: The Crucifixion, detail from the Sancta Sanctorum reliquary box, Vatican Museum, Syria or Palestine, sixth century

This image is then at a later date refracted into two images: that of the dead Christ and that of the resurrection. However, the images of the "resurrection," the "Anastasis," do not in fact depict the crucified Jesus rising out of the tomb but rather his raising of Adam and Eve, representing the whole human race (for instance, Image 5).

In Accordance with the Scriptures

Image 5: The Anastasis, Istanbul, Church in Chora, commissioned by Theodore Metochites, 1310–1317 CE

The apparent anomaly of this is such that these images are often described—mistakenly—as "the harrowing of hell."[20] Indeed, in some of the earliest depictions it is labelled simply as "The Resurrection of Adam" (Image 6).

---

20. See Kartsonis, *Anastasis*, 4, 6: "But any designation of the subject matter of this iconography as the Descent or Harrowing of Hell misrepresents and distorts the message of the chosen label Anastasis. The title and subject matter of this image refer, not to the Descent of Christ into Hades, Limbo, or Inferno, but to the rising of Christ and his raising of the dead. . . . Thus in the image of the Anastasis, Adam stands for Everyman."

Image 6: The Anastasis (of Adam), the Chludov Psalter (Historical Museum, Moscow, ms. gr. 129, 63v), Byzantine, ninth century

This is how Paul, at the beginning of Romans (1:2–4), speaks of the Son: the one promised through the prophets in the scriptures "came to be" (γενομένου) of the seed of David according to the flesh and was "designated [ὁρισθέντος] Son of God in power according to the Spirit of holiness by resurrection of the dead" (ἐξ ἀναστάσεως νεκρῶν; not "from the dead," as is it regularly mistranslated). As Crossan notes, referring to this passage and its connection to 1 Corinthians 15:13, "Christ's Resurrection and the universal resurrection stand or fall together: 'if there is no resurrection of the dead (*anastasis nekrōn*), then Christ has not been raised.'"[21] The iconography of the Anastasis, depicting Christ with his arms outstretched, standing on the doors of Hades placed crosswise, drawing all to himself, alludes most graphically to the words of Christ, in the Gospel of John, speaking about his ascent upon the cross: "When I am lifted up from the earth, I will draw all to myself"—that is, on the cross (John 12:32; see esp. Image 7).

Image 7: The Crucifixion and Resurrection, the Princeton Psalter (Ps 8:7–10, recto), 1090–1100

---

21. Crossan and Crossan, *Resurrecting Easter*, 174.

This is exactly what we have seen in Athanasius. When turning to the resurrection of the body, he makes no mention of the resurrectional appearances of Christ as described in the Gospels (just as he does not refer to the birth narratives) but rather points to the raising of those who now have taken up the faith of the cross to be the body of Christ: It is indeed "the one on the cross," as he affirms, who is the Lord and Savior, the Word of God.

Similarly with regard to the feast of the Nativity, that which we unthinkingly equate with the "incarnation." The most striking feature of Athanasius's treatise is that it makes no mention of, or even allusion to, the birth narratives in Matthew and Luke. But then, when Athanasius wrote *On the Incarnation*, the church in Alexandria did not as yet celebrate a feast for the Nativity of Christ.[22] By the early third century, the coincidence of Nisan 14 with March 25 had already been noted in Rome, and the dating of the birth of Christ to December 25 appears a century later, in what might seem to be an unusual place: The earliest authentic document to give this as the date of the birth of Christ is the *Depositio martyrum* (354 CE), a list of martyrs honored in Rome arranged by the date of their death. It opens with the simple statement: "Christ is born on the eighth of the Calends of January, in Bethlehem of Judea."[23] As Susan Roll notes, it is striking that this statement "appears at the head of the calendar, marking its starting point and thus indicating some importance attached to the event that the year begins from this point."[24] However, while she recognizes that "the prevailing mentality is that the martyrs' deathdate is their birthday into heaven and thus to be celebrated," it is not necessarily the case, as she holds that "this seems to be contradicted by the appearance of the fleshly birth of Christ at the head of the calendar, with no listing of his passion and death."[25]

---

22. See Talley, *Origins of the Liturgical Year*, 140–41. According to John Cassian, the Egyptians celebrate the feast of Epiphany on January 6, and this feast commemorated both the baptism of the Lord and his birth in the flesh (*Conference* 10.2.1, written 418-427 CE), though in the fourth century the feast of Epiphany was exclusively focused on Christ's baptism so that the sixteenth of the *Canons of Athanasius* (of disputed attribution, but dating from the second half of the fourth century) does not even mention the nativity. See Riedel and Crum, *Canons of Athanasius*, 26–27.

23. See Roll, *Origins of Christmas*, 79–84. The connection between Nisan 14 and March 25 is made on the Paschal Tables at the foot of a statue, a Roman copy of a Greek woman philosopher, dating to 222–235 CE. On this, see also Talley, *Origins of the Liturgical Year*, 9–10 (for notes, see 71). Plates of the statue and tables are included in Brent, *Hippolytus and the Roman Church*, plates 1–4.

24. Roll, *Origins of Christmas*, 84.

25. Roll, *Origins of Christmas*, 84; cf. 75.

That the death-day of the martyrs is understood to be their birth—not a "new birth" or a "spiritual birth," but simply their birth—is indeed pervasive in early Christianity.[26] We can see it, for instance, early on in the letter of Ignatius of Antioch to the Christians in Rome, imploring them not to interfere with his coming martyrdom:

> Birth-pangs are upon me [Ὁ δὲ τοκετός μοι ἐπίκειται]. Grant this to me, brethren: hinder me not from living, do not wish me to die. . . . Allow me to receive the pure light; when I will have arrived there, I will be a human being. Allow me to be an imitator of the passion of my God. (Ign. *Rom.* 6)

Not only is he not yet born, but he is not yet living and even not yet human! Another example from later in the second century is the way in which those Christians who had previously denied their faith were encouraged by the witness of others to return to the arena:

> And there was great joy for Virgin Mother in receiving alive those who she had miscarried as dead [ὡς νεκροὺς ἐξέτρωσε], for through them many who had denied retraced their steps and were again conceived and brought to life [ἀνεμετροῦντο καὶ ἀνεκυΐσκοντο καὶ ἀνεζωπυροῦντο] and learnt to witness. (*Hist. Eccl.* 5.1.45–46)

The trials of their martyrdom are their conception and birth-pangs, resulting in their birth into life. Given what we have seen in the previous chapter about the distinction between animation by a mortal breath and vivification in the life-giving Spirit, it might be helpful to return to the conceptual distinction, suggested there, between coming-to-be (*genesis*) and birth (*gennēsis*).[27] What comes to be is animated and necessarily mortal, for all that comes to be in time passes away in time; birth, on the other hand, is only ever birth into life, the life that Christ has come to give and which is received by being "an imitator of the passion of my God." Who the virgin mother is, through whom such a birth occurs, we will consider in the next

---

26. See Machabée, "Life and Death"; Behr, "Our Mother Church."

27. The two words are derived from different verbs: γένεσις, though it can be used for birth, is derived γίνομαι, "to come to be," "to happen"; γέννησις is derived from γεννάω, "to beget." For a very sophisticated, but later, reflection on these two terms, see Maximos, *Ad. Thal.* 61. For a very different, but profound, phenomenological reflection on the relationship between birth and life, see Henry, *I Am the Truth*, e.g., 59–60: "In the world, according to Christianity, no birth is possible. . . . To be born is not to come into the world. To be born is to come into life. . . . To come into life means to come from life, starting from it, in such a way that life is not birth's point of arrival, as it were, but its point of departure."

chapter, and in the final chapter what it means for Ignatius to say that only in this way will he become a human being.

The background for this early Christian understanding of death as birth is probably the designation of Christ as "the firstborn of the dead" by both Paul and John (Col 1:18; Rev 1:5).[28] It is evident also in Peter's speech on the day of Pentecost—when the life-giving Spirit is poured upon all flesh—for he does not simply proclaim that Jesus of Nazareth had risen but that "God raised him from the dead having loosened the birth-pangs of death [τὰς ὠδῖνας τοῦ θανάτου], because it was not possible for him to be held by it" (Acts 2:24). And further, John has the risen Christ describe himself to the Laodiceans as "the Amen, the faithful and true witness [martyr], the beginning [ἀρχή] of God's creation" (Rev 3:14).

The scriptural background for seeing the passion of Christ as a conception followed by birth—a birth, moreover, that extends to others—would seem to be the connection between the fourth hymn of the suffering servant (Isa 52:13—53:12) and the following verse, a connection already evident in Paul's Letter to the Galatians. "When the fullness of time had come," God did *not* send his Son *to be born* of a woman, as the verse is often read, but rather "God sent his Son, who had come to be [γενόμενον] from a woman, who had come to be under the law, to redeem those under the law, so that we might receive adoption" (Gal 4:4). God's sending of his Son—not to be born of a woman, but for redemption, that is, to the cross—has enabled all those who, although heirs, were but children, in slavery to the elemental spirits of the universe until the determined time, to receive adoption and their inheritance—"no longer a slave but a son, and if a son then an heir"—so that, with the Spirit of God's Son in their hearts, they can all call upon God as "Abba Father" (Gal 4:1–3, 5–7). After exhorting his readers not to return back to the elemental spirits and describing himself as being "again in travail [πάλιν ὠδίνω] until Christ be formed in you" (Gal 4:19), Paul presents an allegory of the two sons of Abraham, one born in slavery, the other in freedom through a promise. In contrast to the slave Hagar, corresponding to the present Jerusalem, "the Jerusalem above is free and she is our mother," Paul says, backing this up with the words from Isa 54:1, "Rejoice, O barren one who does not bear, break forth in singing you who are not in travail [ὠδίνουσα], for the children of the desolate one are more than the children of her that is married" (Gal 4:22–27). Read as

---

28. It is possible that behind this use of the term "firstborn" lies Exodus 12–13, the consecration of all the firstborn following Passover and the eating of the Passover lamb.

following the most important scriptural (OT) text regarding the passion of Christ, the fourth hymn of the suffering servant, this verse (Isa 54:1) thus speaks of the opening of the barren womb by the passion of Christ (as we will see further in the next chapter), the womb in which the martyrs are born into life, something anticipated by "being buried with him by baptism into death . . . united with him in a death like his," so as to rise with him, when finally dead, "in the newness of life" (Rom 6:1–11).

The risen Christ Jesus is thus "the firstborn of many brethren" (Rom 8:29), but he is also "the head of the body, the church; the beginning [ἀρχή], the firstborn of the dead" (Col 1:18; cf. Eph 1:22–23). Or, as we saw Dalferth put it, this is not simply the "resurrection of *Jesus*" but the "resurrection of Jesus *Christ*." That Christians are indeed the body of Christ is no loose analogy or metaphor for Paul. He makes the identification without qualification: "You are the body of Christ and individually members of it," all, that is, who "by the one Spirit were baptized into the one body" (1 Cor 12:27, 13). As members of his body, they depend for their life and being upon their head; it is by holding fast to this head that "the whole body, nourished and knit together through its joints and ligaments, grows with a growth that is from God" (Col 2:19). As members of this body, Christians also depend upon one another: "We, though many, are one body in Christ, and individually members of one another" (Rom 12:5). The grace given to each is for the benefit of the one body, so that everything is to be done in love for the building up of the one body (1 Cor 12–13). The crucified and risen Jesus of Nazareth is indeed *the* Christ, but he is also the head of the body *of Christ*, the church.

But this also means, in turn, as Ignatius strikingly put it, regarding the cross and the body of Christ:

> through it [the cross], in his passion, he invites you to be parts of his body, as a head cannot be born without body-parts, because God promises unity, which he himself is. (Ign. *Trall.* 11.2)[29]

The birth of Jesus *Christ*, begun in the death-defeating, life-giving death of Jesus and the "resurrection of *Jesus*" as "the firstborn of the dead," is thus brought to term and deliverance in the birth of the whole body—the head together with the members of his body, the firstborn together with his brethren—by their sharing in his life-giving death, resulting in the "resurrection

---

29. δι' οὗ ἐν τῷ πάθει αὐτοῦ προσκαλεῖται ὑμᾶς ὄντας μέλη αὐτοῦ· οὐ δύναται οὖν κεφαλὴ χωρὶς γεννηθῆναι ἄνευ μελῶν, τοῦ θεοῦ ἕνωσιν ἐπαγγελλομένου, ὅ ἐστιν αὐτός.

of Jesus *Christ*." And as he is, moreover, "the beginning of God's creation," it is in the resurrection of the whole body that God's creation is thus itself finally brought to completion. As the *Martyrology of Jerome* (in the version of Tallaght) puts it: On March 25, "Our Lord Jesus Christ was crucified, and conceived, and the world created"—in that order![30]

Regarding the infancy narratives in Matthew and Luke, we should perhaps recall Dalferth's other point, that the narratives of the New Testament are "no more and no less than interpretations of the resurrection message as proclaimed in the events of Jesus's life."[31] Raymond Brown makes the same point in his studies on the infancy narratives: "The story of Jesus' conception is no longer just an item of popular biography; it is the vehicle of the good news of salvation; in short, it is gospel. . . . The process [of arriving at these birth narratives] was literally an interpretative one of reading back later insights into the birth stories, and those later insights involved an adult Christ who had died and risen."[32] That the infancy narratives stand apart in a distinctive manner from the narratives that follow is evident from the way in which the revelation given in them appears to no longer be known thereafter. The infancy narratives, much like the first eighteen verses of the Gospel of John, should rather be thought of as a prologue. According to Aristotle, a *prooemion* in the case of a speech, a prologue for poetry, and a prelude for flute playing "are all beginnings and, as it were, pathmakers for what follows" (*Rhet.* 3.14.1); they should include the keynote and attach the main subject, so giving enough information as to enable readers or hearers to understand the theme and its development. This means, as Jean Zumstein puts it, in relation to John's Prologue: "This opening word does not place itself on the same level as the following narrative; rather, it assumes a prior reflection about that narrative. The meta-reflective nature of the Prologue marks its intratextual relationship with the narrative, which properly begins [in John] in 1:19."[33] The same goes for the infancy narratives: as an overture to an opera, they anticipate all that is to come, in this case describing the gospel of the crucified and risen one as nothing other than a birth, which it indeed is.

---

30. *Martyrology of Tallaght*, 27; cf. *Martyrologium Hieronymianum*, 159. For the broader cosmic implications, see Chupungo, *Cosmic Elements of Christian Passover*.

31. Dalferth, *Crucified and Risen*, 24.

32. Brown, *Adult Christ at Christmas*, 8. More fully, see Brown, *Birth of the Messiah*.

33. Zumstein, "Intratextuality and Intertextuality," 123.

In Accordance with the Scriptures

The connection between the passion and the birth is again clearly presented in the iconography for the birth of Christ. The earliest depictions of the nativity come in two forms, either the infant Jesus wrapped in swaddling clothes lying in a manger with an ox and ass gazing on him with a star above (alluding to Num 24:17; see Image 8), or the Adoration of the Magi, three in number, bearing gifts for a dead, divine Lord, as seen in a third-century fresco in the Catacomb of Priscilla and on sarcophagi and ivory pyxes from the fourth century and fifth century (see Image 9).[34]

Image 8: The Nativity, marble relief on a gravestone at Sangri on Naxos (Byzantine Museum in Athens, BXM 312), ca. 400 CE

34. See Varalis, "Nativity of Christ on Late Antique Ivories."

The Paschal Christ

Image 9: The Adoration of the Magi, detail from a sarcophagus
in the cemetery of St. Agnes, Rome, fourth century

The mosaic in the Basilica of Santa Maria Maggiore in Rome (Image 10) is particularly striking, depicting an infant Christ with a cross in his halo, receiving the gifts from the Magi while sitting upright on the lap of the Virgin, who is herself seated upon a throne; it is an enthronement scene (Image 10). This enthronement is even more dramatically depicted in the Ivory panel in the British Museum (Image 11), where the Virgin and Child are seated, facing forward, surrounded by the Magi and an angel bearing a cross, while in the lower register (and in a much smaller scale) there is the infant in the crib with the ox and ass standing alongside.

In Accordance with the Scriptures

Image 10: The Adoration of the Magi, mosaic in the Basilica of Santa Maria Maggiore, Rome, ca. 435

The Paschal Christ

Image 11: The Adoration of the Magi, ivory panel,
British Museum, London (1904, 0702.1)

From the sixth century (for instance, on the Lateran Reliquary box, Image 12), we begin to see what comes to be the standard iconographic depiction of the nativity. The infant, already with a cross in his halo, is wrapped in swaddling clothes, like a corpse, and placed in a manger, shaped as a tomb or altar, in a cave. The Virgin and cave form one artistic shape, just as the crucified Christ had been placed in a new-hewn tomb in which no one had been laid—that is, a virgin tomb, owned by (the other) Joseph (see Image 13). "To the tomb, in which no body had been laid before or after," as Augustine observes, following the order of identification, "corresponds the womb in which he was conceived, where no mortal body was sown before or after" (*Trin.* 4.2.9).

Image 12: The Nativity of Christ, detail from the Sancta Sanctorum reliquary box, Vatican Museum, Syria or Palestine, sixth century

The Paschal Christ

Image 13: The Nativity of Christ, mosaic in the Church in Daphni, Greece, ca. 1100 CE

The differences between the "restructured" christological grammar proposed by Dalferth, on the one hand, and what we have seen in Athanasius's *On the Incarnation* and in the development of liturgical feasts and iconography, on the other, derive in large part from different starting points, or, in terms of the previous chapter, different ways of thinking about or figuring scripture. Dalferth starts with our present theological framework, with its distinct elements now thought of as different historical events (incarnation, crucifixion, resurrection), reading scripture now in a linear manner (with an Old Testament followed by a New Testament, beginning with the birth of Jesus), and with the predicaments into which we are then led (how to give full weight to Christ's humanity and divinity and yet the unity of person), with theories of en- and an-hypostasis, all of which, as Dalferth argues, echoing many others, ultimately fail. What we have proposed starts with the paschal mystery, the unveiling of scripture by the cross to reveal the eternal mystery, and then traces how the different aspects or moments of this mystery are then brought into distinct focus and feasts within a liturgical calendar, yet always bearing the imprint of the paschal mystery itself. Dalferth's reconstructive proposal that we should always begin by recognizing that confessional statements always already speak of "the Jesus Christ who was raised from the dead" is indeed salutary. But rather than trying to put the various elements (as we think we already know them) back together again, if we reflect on how the various elements of Christian theology were originally (and for centuries) all held together in the paschal mystery and refracted, from that pure white light, into the spectrum of theological loci and liturgical feasts yet still bearing their original paschal imprint, we might find a greater and more dynamic coherence, such that the problems we are attempting to resolve look very different: The paschal death overcomes death by turning death into a birth into life (*gennēsis*), contrasted with mere mortal coming-into-being (*genesis*), and likewise showing incarnation to be the birth of the (whole) body of Christ.

"You are my Son, today have I begotten you"

When Paul preached the gospel in Antioch of Pisidia, according to Acts, he proclaimed: "We bring you good news that what God has promised to the fathers this he has fulfilled to us their children by raising Jesus; as it is written in the second Psalm, 'You are my Son, today have I begotten you'" (Acts 13:32–33; Ps 2:7). What, however, is meant by the statement that the crucified and risen Jesus is begotten of God and is so begotten "*today*"?

This was, of course, the subject of great debate in the fourth century, much of which focused on the verses from Proverbs: "The Lord created me [ἔκτισέν με] as the beginning of his ways, for the sake of his works.... before the mountains were established and before all the hills he begets me [γεννᾷ με]" (8:22–25). For Athanasius, unlike his opponents, these verses pointed to a clear distinction between begetting and creating, one that became standard for Nicene theology ("begotten not made"), and relatively easy to grasp. As Athanasius succinctly put it,

> God's creating is second to his begetting, for the Son is proper [ἴδιον] to and truly from that divine and everlastingly existent essence, whereas those things that are from the will have come to be constituted from outside [ἔξωθεν], and are made though his proper Offspring, who is from [the essence]. (*C. Ar.* 2.2.6)

That Christ is the Son means that God is Father, and as God creates through his Son, creating is "second" to begetting, so, as Origen had put it, the title "Father" is "older" in God than that of "Almighty" and "Maker" (*Princ.*

1.2.10). The order of the words in the creedal confession—One God Father Almighty Maker of heaven and earth—is a logical progression.[35]

Yet what is the content of this "begetting" of the Son and the "creating" of the world that are thus contrasted? Later in the fourth century, Gregory the Theologian warned that if his opponents were to explain to him the unbegottenness of the Father and he, in turn, were to "give a physiological account of the birth of the Son," and the Spirit's proceeding, "we will both go mad for prying into the secrets of God."[36] Athanasius, however, did give an account, a definition even, of the "begetting" of the Son, and one that, intriguingly, maintains not only the distinction but also an intimate connection between the Son's relationship to the Father and the relation between created beings and God. He reports that those who resisted, saying that the Son is from the essence of the Father, were fearful lest it result in a division of that essence, so they resorted to saying that the Son is such as he is by participation. But Athanasius asks them, "Of what is he a participant?" (*C. Ar.* 1.15.4): it cannot be a participation in the Spirit, for the Spirit "receives" from the Son (cf. John 16:14), nor can it be by participating "in something external provided by the Father," for, in that case, there would be an intervening principle between the Father and the Son. And so, Athanasius points out, "what-is-participated [τὸ μετεχόμενον] is not external, but from the essence of the Father" (*C. Ar.* 1.15.6). Yet if this "what-is-participated" is other than the Son, that would again interpose something between the Father and Son. And so, Athanasius then concludes:

> We must say that what is "from the essence of the Father" and proper to him is entirely the Son. For it is the same thing to say that God is wholly "participated" and that he "begets" [τὸ γὰρ ὅλως »μετέχεσθαι« τὸν θεὸν ἴσον ἐστὶ λέγειν ὅτι καὶ »γεννᾷ«·]; for what does "to beget" signify, except a Son? And so all things participate in the Son himself [αὐτοῦ γοῦν τοῦ υἱοῦ μετέχει τὰ πάντα] according to the grace of the Spirit coming from him; from this it is clear that the Son himself participates of nothing [ὅτι αὐτὸς μὲν ὁ υἱὸς οὐδενὸς μετέχει], but that-which-is-participated-in from the Father that is the Son [τὸ δὲ ἐκ τοῦ πατρὸς μετεχόμενον, τοῦτο ἐστιν ὁ υἱός]. For, as participating in the Son himself, we are said to participate of God, and this is what Peter said, "that you may be partakers of the divine nature" [2 Pet 1:4]; as the Apostle says also, "Do you not know that you are a temple of God?" [1 Cor

---

35. See Behr, "One God Father Almighty."
36. Gregory of Nazianzus, *Oration* 31.8.

3:16] and, "We are the temple of the living God" [2 Cor 6:16]. And seeing the Son, we see the Father [cf. John 14:9]; for the thought and comprehension of the Son is knowledge of the Father, because he is the proper Offspring from his essence. And since no one of us would ever call "being-participated-in" a passion or division of God's essence (for it has been granted and acknowledged, that God is participated-in, and to be participated-in is the same thing as to beget [ταὐτὸν εἶναι μετέχεσθαι καὶ γεννᾶν]), therefore that which is begotten is neither a passion nor division of that blessed essence. (*C. Ar.* 1.16)[37]

Athanasius's point, in this fascinating passage, is that while human beings participate in the Son by the grace of the Spirit, and in so doing participate in God himself, the Son does not participate (for that would imply a point of origin other than the Father): he is, rather, "that-which-is-participated-in from the Father." The difference between human participation in God and the participation in the Father that *is* the Son does not turn upon the legitimacy of using the language of participation but how that language is used. This distinction, moreover, doesn't rest upon a belief that there is a part of the human being (say, for instance, the "body" as opposed to the "intellect") that does not, or cannot, participate in God, or that there is a "part" of God, as it were, in which we do not participate, for participating in God we become "partakers of the divine nature." But neither is it *simply* a question of the "whence"—the principle that we participate in God from the outside, whereas the Son has no point of origin other than the Father, from which he might be said to have come to participate in God. Rather, the distinction is that while we come to participate in the Son, by the grace of the Spirit, the Son is "that-which-is-participated-in from the Father's essence," and this, moreover, is his begetting. Yet this language describing the begetting of the Son also implies those who are participating in the Son. Indeed, it is on the basis of the scriptural affirmations that we are to be "partakers of the divine nature" and the "temple of God" that Athanasius asserts his claim: while we participate in the Son, the Son participates in nothing; rather, he is "that-which-is-participated-in from the Father," and this *is* his begetting.

For the background for this way of conceptualizing the Son's relation to the Father and our relation to the Father through the Son and the Spirit, in the language and framework of participation, we must look to Origen,

---

37. On this passage, see Anatolios, *Athanasius*, 105–9; Behr, *Nicene Faith*, 236–38.

who had used such terminology as a way of resolving the difficulties of those afraid of proclaiming two Gods. Origen proposes this resolution to their predicament:

> We must say to them that at one time God, with the article, is very God, wherefore also the Savior says in his prayer to the Father, "That they may know you the only true God" [John 17:3]. On the other hand, everything besides the very God, which is made God by participation in his divinity [μετοχῇ τῆς ἐκείνου θεότητος θεοποιούμενον], would more properly not be said to be "*the* God," but "God." To be sure, his "firstborn of every creature" [Col 1:15], inasmuch as he was the first to be with God, drawing divinity into himself [ἅτε πρῶτος τῶι πρὸς τὸν θεὸν εἶναι σπάσας τῆς θεότητος εἰς ἑαυτόν], is more honoured than any other Gods besides him (of whom God is God as it is said, "The God of Gods, the Lord has spoken, and he has called the earth" [Ps 50:1/49:1]). It was by his ministry that they became Gods, for he drew from God that they might be deified, sharing ungrudgingly also with them according to his goodness [διακονήσας τὸ γενέσθαι θεοῖς, ἀπὸ τοῦ θεοῦ ἀρυσά<μενος> εἰς τὸ θεοποιηθῆναι αὐτούς, ἀφθόνως κἀκείνοις κατὰ τὴν αὐτοῦ χρηστότητα μεταδιδούς]. *The* God, therefore, is the true God; the others are Gods formed according to him as images of the prototype. But again, the archetypal image of the many images is *the* Word with *the* God, who was "in the beginning." By being "with *the* God" he always continues to be "God." But he would not have this if he were not with God, and he would not remain God if he did not continue in unceasing contemplation of the depth of the Father [τῷ εἶναι »πρὸς τὸν θεὸν« ἀεὶ μένων »θεός«, οὐκ ἂν δ' αὐτὸ ἐσχηκὼς εἰ μὴ πρὸς θεὸν ἦν, καὶ οὐκ ἂν μείνας θεός, εἰ μὴ παρέμενε τῇ ἀδιαλείπτῳ θέᾳ τοῦ πατρικοῦ βάθους]. (*Comm. John* 2:17–18)

Origen's language of the Son being "God" by participation in the divinity of the very God is certainly turned around by Athanasius: being from the essence of the Father, the Son does not participate in God but is instead that-which-*is*-participated-in. But what is striking is that both explain the Son's relationship to God in terms that also include the Son's relationship to others. For Athanasius, the begetting of the Son is his being "that-which-is-partaken-in from the Father" so that others can become partakers of the divine nature; for Origen, the Son draws divinity into himself to minister it to others, deifying them while himself remaining distinct as "the first to be with God" and thus "the firstborn of every creature." Remaining in this "unceasing contemplation of the depths of the Father," he remains God, ministering divinity to others.

What Origen might mean by this language of "drawing divinity into himself," so as to minister it to others, and "the unceasing contemplation of the depths of the Father" is perhaps made clearer by the analogies he gives in *On First Principles*, written around the same time as this passage from the *Commentary on John* though only preserved in Rufinus's translation. Drawing from Stoic physics, Origen points out that while iron is capable of being both hot or cold, if it is placed in a fire and never removed from it, it burns incessantly, never becoming cold: it has become "wholly fire" (*Princ.* 2.6.6).[38] In the same way, he continues, the soul of Jesus,

> which, like iron in the fire, was placed in the Word forever, in Wisdom forever, in God forever, is God in all that it does, feels, and understands; and therefore it can be called neither alterable or changeable, since, being ceaselessly kindled, it came to possess immutability from its union with the Word of God. To all the saints some warmth of the Word of God must indeed be supposed to have passed; but in this soul it must be believed that the divine fire itself essentially rested, from which some warmth may have passed to others. (*Princ.* 2.6.6)

And then, in addition to this analogy, Origen draws upon scriptural verses to make the same point:

> Finally, the fact that it says, "God, your God, anointed you with the oil of gladness above your fellows" [Ps 45:7/44:8], shows that that soul is anointed in one way, with the oil of gladness, that is, with the Word of God and Wisdom, and his fellows, that is, the holy prophets and apostles, in another way. For they are said to have "run in the fragrance of his ointment" [Song 1:4], while that soul was the vessel containing the ointment itself, of whose glowing heat all the prophets and apostles are made worthy partakers. Therefore, as the fragrance of the ointment is one thing, and the substance of the ointment another, so also Christ is one thing and his fellows another. And just as the vessel itself, which contains the substance of the ointment, can in no way accept any foul smell, yet it is possible that those who participate in its fragrance, if they move a little way from its glowing heat, may accept any foul smell that comes upon them, so also, in the same way, it was impossible

---

38. See especially Alexander of Aphrodisias, *Mixt.* 3.218.1–2, reporting the teaching of Chrysippus.

that Christ, being as it were the very vessel in which was the substance of the ointment, should accept an odour of an opposite kind, while his fellows, in proportion to their proximity to the vessel, will be partakers and receivers of his fragrance. (*Princ.* 2.6.6)

The distinction between Jesus the Christ, the Anointed One, and "his fellows," or "his participants" (τοὺς μετόχους σου, in the LXX of Ps 44:8), is maintained: he is himself the vessel containing the ointment ("the whole fullness of divinity dwells in him bodily," as Paul says in Col 2:9), and it is in its fragrance that his fellows or participants run, sharing in the warmth that he ministers to them.

Returning to the *Commentary on John*, Origen specifies when and how, in the terms of the analogies, the iron enters the fire or the vessel receives the ointment.

> The high exaltation of the Son of Man which occurred when he glorified God in his own death consisted in the fact that he was no longer different from the Word but was the same with him [ἡ δὲ ὑπερύψωσις τοῦ υἱοῦ τοῦ ἀνθρώπου, γενομένη αὐτῷ δοξάσαντι τὸν θεὸν ἐν τῷ ἑαυτοῦ θανάτῳ, αὕτη ἦν, τὸ μηκέτι ἕτερον αὐτὸν εἶναι τοῦ λόγου ἀλλὰ τὸν αὐτὸν αὐτῷ]. For if "he who is joined to the Lord is one spirit" [1 Cor 6:17], so that it is no longer said that "they are two" [Matt 19:6; Gen 2:2], even in the case of this man and the spirit, might we not much more say that the humanity of Jesus became one with the Word [τὸ ἀνθρώπινον τοῦ Ἰησοῦ μετὰ τοῦ λόγου λέγοιμεν γεγονέναι ἕν] when he who did not consider "equality with God" something to be grasped was highly exalted [Phil 2:6, 9], the Word, however, remaining in his own grandeur, or even being restored to it, when he was again with God, God the Word being human [μένοντος δὲ ἐν τῷ ἰδίῳ ὕψει ἢ καὶ ἀποκαθισταμένου ἐπ' αὐτὸ τοῦ λόγου, ὅτε πάλιν ἦν πρὸς τὸν θεόν, θεὸς λόγος ὢν ἄνθρωπος]? (*Comm. John* 32.325–26)

That the identity of the Son of Man with, or rather as, the Word of God is wrought upon the cross reiterates the point we have seen Athanasius concerned to demonstrate, that it is the one who ascended the cross that is the very Word of God. This implies no change in the Word of God, just as the fire does not change when the iron enters into it—with the exception that the fire is now embodied, and so, as embodied (although in a body now known by the properties of the fire), the fire has taken form, to be the image in which the fire can, as it were, see itself and also (and thereby) become accessible to others. The glorification of God by exaltation of the

Son of Man ascending the cross into the heavens provides us, in return or reverse, with the descent of the heavenly fire in the form of the Spirit (cf. Acts 2:3), setting the disciples hearts and minds aflame (cf. Luke 24:32), burning to follow him: "I came to cast fire upon the earth and would that it were already kindled!" (Luke 12:49).[39]

If something like this lies behind Athanasius's description of the Son as "that-which-is-participated-in from the Father" (and is then further developed by Gregory of Nyssa's reflections on Peter's statement that "God has made him both Lord and Christ, this Jesus whom you crucified"),[40] then there is indeed more that can be said regarding Athanasius's statement that this constitutes the Son's begetting. At one point, Origen seems to connect the Son's begetting and his drawing divinity into himself. Commenting on Christ's words that "no one is good but God alone" (Mark 10:18 et par), Origen emphasizes that this should not be taken to imply that the Son and Spirit are not "good." Rather,

> as we have said above, the primal goodness is recognized in the God and Father, from whom both the Son, being begotten, and the Spirit, proceeding, without doubt draw into themselves the nature of his goodness [*sine dubio bonitatis eius naturam in se refert*], which exists in the source, from whom the Son is born and the Spirit proceeds. (*Princ.* 1.2.13)

The Son is not simply begotten from the Father, for if that were the case, he would be a passive outcome of God's activity and thus not "true God of true God." Rather, his being begotten is correlated to his drawing divinity into himself to minister it to others: It is a birth (*gennēsis*) in which the one being born is active, unlike the passivity of coming-into-being (*genesis*).

Moreover, the "today" of the apostolic preaching (Acts 13:32–33; Ps 2:7, cited above) and the odd present tense of Proverbs 8:25 ("before all the hills he begets me") are the basis of the "eternal begetting" of the Son, and not only him. Origen notes the claims of John (in his version) that "everyone who sins is begotten of the devil" and "the one begotten of God does not sin" (1 John 3:8–9), and concludes:

> I will not say that the righteous one is begotten just once by God, but that he is always begotten in each good act in which God begets the righteous one [οὐ γὰρ ἅπαξ ἐρῶ τὸν δίκαιον γεγεννῆσθαι

---

39. See Stang, "Origen's Theology of Fire."

40. Acts 2:36, analyzed in detail by Gregory of Nyssa, *Against Eunomius* 3.3; cf. Radde-Gallwitz, "*Contra Eunomium* III 3"; Behr, *Nicene Faith*, 435–58.

ὑπὸ τοῦ θεοῦ, ἀλλ' ἀεὶ γεννᾶσθαι καθ' ἑκάστην πρᾶξιν ἀγαθήν, ἐν ᾗ γεννᾷ τὸν δίκαιον ὁ θεός]. If then I set before you, with respect to the Savior, that the Father has not begotten the Son and then severed him from his begetting, but always begets him [οὐχὶ ἐγέννησεν ὁ πατὴρ τὸν υἱὸν καὶ ἀπέλυσεν αὐτὸν ὁ πατὴρ ἀπὸ τῆς γενέσεως αὐτοῦ, ἀλλ' ἀεὶ γεννᾷ αὐτόν], I will also present something similar [παραπλήσιον] for the righteous one.... [Heb 1:3; Wis 7:26; 1 John 1:5; 1 Cor 1:24] ... If then, the Savior is always begotten—because of this he also says, "Before all the hills he begets me," and not "before all the hills he has begotten me," but "before all the hills he begets me"—and the Savior is always begotten by the Father [ἀεὶ γεννᾶται ὁ σωτὴρ ὑπὸ τοῦ πατρός], so also, if you possess the "Spirit of adoption" [Rom 8:15], God always begets you in him [ἀεὶ γεννᾷ σε ἐν αὐτῷ ὁ θεὸς] according to each of your works, each of your thoughts. And may one so begotten always be a begotten son of God in Christ Jesus [καὶ γεννώμενος οὕτως γίνῃ ἀεὶ γεννώμενος υἱὸς θεοῦ ἐν Χριστῷ Ἰησοῦ]. (*Hom. Jer.* 9.4)

The distinction between the begetting of Son and our own being begotten of God is not the "eternality" of the former, for such also applies to us; rather, it is *in* Christ Jesus that we receive "the Spirit of adoption" to become ourselves always or eternally begotten of God so that our sonship is only ever based on that of Christ. This begetting or birth (both Christ's and ours "in Christ") is not a one-off, unidirectional act: the righteous one is begotten of God in righteous acts, so holding together both the active and the passive dimensions, leading us, in Christ, to being always or eternally begotten sons and daughters of God in Christ, the Son of God.

Further insight into the nature of this relationship is given in Athanasius's comments on later verses from Proverbs 8: "I was the one in whom he took delight; and each day I was rejoicing in his presence at every moment, when he rejoiced having consummated the world and rejoiced among the sons of men" (8:30–31). According to Athanasius:

> In whom, then, does the Father rejoice, except by seeing himself in his own Image [βλέπων ἑαυτὸν ἐν τῇ ἰδίᾳ εἰκόνι], who is his Word? If he also "rejoiced in the sons of men, having consummated the world" [τὴν οἰκουμένην συντελέσας], as it is written in these same Proverbs, yet this also has the same meaning [ἀλλὰ καὶ τοῦτο τὴν αὐτὴν ἔχει διάνοιαν]. For even thus he rejoiced, joy not being added to him, but seeing again the works that came to be in accordance with his own image, so that even the basis of God's rejoicing is his own Image [εὐφραίνεται γὰρ καὶ οὕτως οὐκ ἐπιγενομένης αὐτῷ

χαρᾶς, ἀλλὰ πάλιν βλέπων κατὰ τὴν ἑαυτοῦ εἰκόνα γενόμενα τὰ ἔργα, ὥστε καὶ τὸ οὕτως χαίρειν τὸν θεὸν τῆς εἰκόνος αὐτοῦ τὴν πρόφασιν εἶναι]. And how does the Son also rejoice, except by seeing himself in the Father? For to say this is the same as to say, "The one who has seen me has seen the Father" and "I am in the Father and the Father is in me" [John 14:9, 10]. (*C. Ar.* 2.82.2–3)

The relationship between God and human beings is again bound up with, and an expression of, the relationship between Father and Son. The delight that the Father has in seeing himself in his own Image is located precisely upon the dynamics of the cross, for "the image of the invisible God" is, according to Paul, precisely the one on the cross, reconciling all things to God and "making peace by the blood of the cross" (Col 1:15, 20). As such, since the basis or occasion for God's delight is his own Image, the delight God also has in his works is not an addition, it "has the same meaning," and so is an extension or, perhaps better, an incorporation. In "the consummation of the world" his works come to be according to his own Image, so God "again sees" his Image and delights similarly so that the basis for this (second) rejoicing is "again" his own Image. The end that is manifested in Christ's elevation upon the cross ("it is finished," John 19:30) is the end to which all creation is called—our end is coterminous though not synchronous.

This rejoicing of the Father in seeing himself in his own Image, spoken of by Athanasius, can be given a more concrete content by returning once again to Origen. Inverting our usual reading of Philippians 2, in which the taking of "the form of a servant" is seen as laying aside "the form of God," Origen asserts:

> We must say that the goodness of Christ appeared greater and more divine and truly in obedience with the image of the Father when "he humbled himself and became obedient unto death, even death on a cross," than if "he had considered being equal to God robbery" [Phil 2:8, 6] and had not been willing to become a servant for salvation of the world. (*Comm. John* 1.231)

When, as Origen puts it, the Son of Man is exalted by glorifying God through his own death to become one with the Word, the consuming fire that is God, I suggested earlier, takes concrete form as "the image of the invisible God" so that the Father can "see himself in his own image," as Athanasius put it, and so rejoice. In Christ's own words: "For this reason [διὰ τοῦτο] the Father loves me, because I lay down my life [τὴν ψυχήν μου] that I may take it again" (John 10:17); a love that is traced back to God himself, for "this is how God loves [οὕτως γὰρ ἠγάπησεν ὁ θεὸς] the world, that he gave his unique Son" (John 3:16); *this* is the action by which the Father is glorified and Christ in turn is glorified by the Father with the glory that they shared before the world was (John 17); *this* is the love that God is (1 John 4:7), and the love that others are invited to share in the same way (John 15:13, etc.). It is in the love that Jesus Christ shows by voluntarily and actively going to the cross, in the Gospel of John, that God "sees himself," the Father in the Son.

There are two further points that should be made. First, that while the difference between the "whence" is certainly important (that we, having been created by the will of God, come to participate in God from the outside, while the Son is "from the essence of the Father"), the difference is also, and perhaps more fundamentally, between "coming-into-being" (*genesis*), in which we were (necessarily) passive and mortal, and "birth" (*gennēsis*) into life. Not only is Christ's human birth active and purposive (he willed to become human, for us and our salvation), but this active purposiveness also characterizes his being begotten from the Father. This is not a unidirectional and temporally discrete act but his being "that-which-is-participated-in from the Father" by drawing divinity into himself to minister it to others, by ascending the cross to draw down the Spirit as tongues of fire. In so doing, he opens the womb in which we too can now be born, actively, into life, "being born from above" (γεννηθῇ ἄνωθεν, John 3:3), by our taking up the cross as well. By following him, we thus change the ground of our existence from necessity and mortality to one of freedom and self-offering love, thereby being constituted as eternally begotten sons of God and constituting ourselves as living human beings, as Ignatius saw and to which we will return in chapter 4, by giving our "Let it be!": "You are Gods, sons of the Most-High; but you will die like human beings" (Ps 82:6–7/81:6–7).

Second, if, as Athanasius puts it, Christ's being "that-which-is-participated-in from the Father" is his being begotten, we can now see the full force of his interpretation of the passage from Colossians regarding the one on the cross being "the image of the invisible God" (Col 1:15). The Father rejoices in his own Image and, with the same meaning, also rejoices in those who come to be in accordance with his own Image, if for no other reason than that the one who is the Image of the invisible God is also "the head of the body, the church, the beginning, the first-born of the dead" (Col 1:18). This pattern of thinking has deep roots within the scriptures. Israel is "my firstborn Son" (Exod 4:22; Jer 31:9), yet what applies to Israel as a whole also holds for all the sons and daughters of Israel, for "you are sons of the Lord your God" (Deut 14:1; cf. 32:5, 19; Isa 43:6). So, too, Christ is God's "proper" or "own" (ἴδιος, Rom 8:32) or "unique" (μονογενής, John 1:14, 18; 3:16, 18) Son (titles not extended to others), given up by God for all, so "the sufferings of the present time" is now creation "groaning in travail," awaiting "the unveiling of the sons of God," "the children of God," that is, those awaiting for "the adoption of sons," those who are destined to be conformed to "his Son," so that he might be "the first-born of many brethren" (Rom 8:18–32) and, as *the* Christ, head of the body *of* Christ. "Incarnation," as we have seen, is an event of birth and incorporation—the iron in the fire and the fire in the iron—of both the risen Jesus, as the head of the body, and the birth of the body of Jesus *Christ*. It is, moreover, the "completion of the world" (Prov 8:31), in which God rejoices, for as with the iron in the fire, becoming "wholly fire" in all that it does, feels, and understands, so the end to which we are called, when God is "all in all," is one where God will indeed be everything in everyone. We "will no longer sense anything else apart from God; [we] will think God, see God, hold God; God will be the mode and measure of [our] every movement; and thus 'God' will be 'all' to [us]" (*Princ.* 3.6.3; 1 Cor 15:28). Love alone remains, the love that is God (cf. 1 Cor 13:8; 1 John 4:8).

3

The Virgin Mother

IF, WITH THE PROCLAMATION of the gospel, death is no longer simply the natural correlate of our coming into being (*genesis*), in an existence animated by a fleeting breath, but a voluntary birth (*gennēsis*) into a life no longer subject to death, then a maternal womb is required. A clear example of the awareness of this is seen in the "Letter of the Christians of Vienne and Lyons to those in Asia and Phrygia," probably written by Irenaeus of Lyons, following the pogrom of Christians in the area of Vienne and Lyons in the year 177 CE.[1] The heroine of the whole account is the young slave girl, Blandina. More space is devoted to her and her ordeals than any other; she is named, while her mistress, also a Christian, remains unnamed. As a young, female slave, she was the lowest of the low in ancient societal terms but thereby also the perfect vessel for the strength of God made manifest in her (cf. 2 Cor 12:9). Indeed, although brutalized extensively by the gladiators, it was they who were beaten by her: they were defeated while she remained steadfast in her confession of being a Christian (*Hist. Eccl.* 5.1.18–19). Even more, the other Christians in the arena looking at her suspended upon a stake (ἐπὶ ξύλου), in the words of the letter, "beheld with their outward eyes, through the sister, him who was crucified for them" (*Hist. Eccl.* 5.1.41–42): she embodies Christ. Others, however, were not so steadfast but abandoned their confession. Nevertheless, seeing the resolve

---

1. The letter can be found in *Hist. Eccl.* 5.1–4. On this letter, see Nautin, *Lettres et écrivains chrétiens*, 33–61.

of Blandina and Attulus, another young figure, they returned to bear witness. Or, rather, as the letter puts it:

> Through their [Blandina's and Attulus's] continued life the dead were made alive, and the martyrs showed favour to those who had failed to witness. And there was great joy for Virgin Mother in receiving alive those whom she had miscarried as dead [ὡς νεκροὺς ἐξέτρωσε], for through them many who had denied retraced their steps and were again conceived and brought to life [ἀνεμετροῦντο καὶ ἀνεκυΐσκοντο καὶ ἀνεζωπυροῦντο] and learnt to witness; and now living and strengthened they went to the judgement seat. (*Hist. Eccl.* 5.1.45–46)

Those who had previously abandoned their confession and so were considered to be still-born—dead—were encouraged by the witness, the *martyria*, of Blandina and Attulus to return to their confession and so were born into life. And in this the virgin mother rejoices. It is not here specified who this virgin mother is; it must have been such a commonplace designation that it is presumed that we already know. As we will see, however, there is no doubt that it refers to the church.

Paul

The proclamation of the gospel is intimately bound up with language of birth and begetting from the beginning. Paul only mentions in passing "a woman" from whom Christ "came to be" (γενόμενον, Gal 4:4). However, he uses the language of receiving the Word and bearing or begetting Christ, and he uses it to great effect. Having preached the gospel—that Christ died and rose in accordance with the scriptures—giving birth to faith in Christ, a faith that comes from hearing (Rom 10:17), Paul sees his task as nourishing the new Christians: he likens himself to "a nurse taking care of her children" and exhorting his community "like a father with his children" (1 Thess 2:7, 11). More dramatically, he states that "I begot [ἐγέννησα] you in Christ Jesus through the Gospel" (1 Cor 4:15). Addressing the Galatians in even more dramatic terms, he speaks of himself as a mother giving birth to Christ: "My little children, with whom I am again in travail [ὠδίνω], until Christ be formed in you!" (Gal 4:19). Paul's converts are those who have been born in Christ Jesus through the gospel and are now having Christ formed in them; indeed, they are "the body of Christ and individually members of it" (1 Cor 12:27), and they are "the one body" of Christ (Col

3:15) by living under "the head of the body, the church, the one who is the *archē* [principle, source, beginning], the firstborn of the dead," that is the Lord Jesus Christ in whom "the whole fullness of divinity dwells bodily" (Col 1:18–19; 2:9). Christ has been "given to be the head over all things for the church, which is his body, the fullness of him who fills all in all" (Eph 1:22–23). And the "profound mystery" of the man leaving his parents and joining to his wife to become one flesh (Gen 2:24) refers, according to Paul, "to Christ and the church" (Eph 5:32). And so, writing to the Corinthians, Paul can say that he has betrothed them to Christ, that he might "present [them] as a pure virgin to her one husband" (2 Cor 11:2).

In portraying the proclamation of the gospel in terms of giving birth to Christians, to those who respond to the word of the cross in faith, forming Christ in them such that they become members of the body of Christ, Paul is drawing upon various scriptural themes. We have already seen him allude to Genesis for the idea that the church, the body of Christ, is also the spouse of Christ, something we will see further developed later. The language of begetting, however, would seem to be drawn from Isa 54:1. Although Paul has not, in the passages mentioned so far, alluded to this verse—a connection that is, however, made by those who followed him—he does cite the verse to speak of "our mother" when he takes Gen 16 and 21 as speaking allegorically, contrasting two modes of childbirth:

> These women are two covenants: one is from Mount Sinai, bearing children for slavery; she is Hagar—now Hagar is Mount Sinai in Arabia; she corresponds to the present Jerusalem, for she is in slavery with her children—while the Jerusalem above is free, she is our mother, for it is written "Rejoice O barren one, who did not bear; break forth into singing and cry aloud, you who have not been in travail; for the children of the desolate one will be more than the children of her that is married," says the Lord. (Gal 4:24–26; Isa 54:1)

This passage from Isaiah of course follows on from what was probably the most important scriptural text for understanding the person and the passion of Christ: the "fourth hymn of the suffering servant" (Isa 52:13—53:12), which speaks of the suffering of the servant, bruised for our iniquities and pouring out his soul unto death. Following Christ's own birth as the firstborn of the dead, the barren woman now becomes a virgin mother—the heavenly mother, the free Jerusalem, giving birth, freely, to a multitude of children; she is the one in or through whom we are born in following

Christ by taking up the cross. A way is opened up for a voluntary birth (*gennēsis*) into life rather than the involuntary coming-into-being (*genesis*) in mortality.

It is striking that, although modern scholarship takes Isa 54:1 as beginning a different oracle, the only time that the passage about the Suffering Servant (Isa 52:13—53:12) is read in the Byzantine liturgical tradition, it is followed, immediately, as a conclusion, by Isa 54:1.[2] The Passion Gospels having previously been read on Holy Thursday Matins, standing at the foot of the cross, the "Rite of Entombment" is celebrated at Vespers, reenacting how Joseph of Arimathea took down the body of Christ from the cross and placed it in the new-hewn tomb, where no one had ever yet been laid (cf. Luke 23:53 et par). The passion of Christ is, as it were, the catalyst opening the tomb, the womb of the barren one, who now gives birth to many children, for it is into the death of Christ that Christians are baptized, in order to rise to life in him (cf. Rom 6:3–11). The final part of the drama was the procession into the building of the newly baptized on Holy Saturday (one of the key days for baptism in the early centuries): with many children now entering to celebrate the mystery of Christ's pascha, the previously barren woman, now a mother, rejoices.

John

Further scriptural background for the imagery of the mother is deployed by John in his gospel. Our examination of how the end is read in terms of the beginning, in the first chapter, provides the framework for this, as does the hint provided by Ignatius—that only by following Christ in his passion will he be born into life and become a human being—which we saw briefly in the second chapter and will explore further in the following chapter. That John has Genesis in mind when composing his gospel is clear from the opening words, "In the beginning." The final word of Christ upon the cross, as I have argued elsewhere and we will see further in the next chapter, alludes back to the distinction in the way that the actions of God

---

2. Janeras, *Le Vendredi-Saint*, 214–17, gives as the first witness of this the Evergetis Typikon (eleventh century). However, as Daniel Galadza pointed out in personal correspondence, the edition to the Evergetis Typikon used by Janeras (that of Dmitrievskii, *Opisanie*, 1:552) in fact only lists the incipit, as is customary in typika, but not the desinit; the most one can conclude is that Isa 54:1 was included in the reading from some point after the twelfth century.

The Virgin Mother

are described in Genesis 1.[3] Scripture opens with God speaking everything into being by an imperative—let it be, it is, it is good—mapping out the opening days. Then, having set the stage, as it were, God announces, with a subjunctive: "Let us make the human being in our image after our likeness" (Gen 1:26). This is a project; indeed, it is the only project that God specifically deliberates upon and announces in this way. That Christ's last word from the cross in the Gospel of John—"it is finished" (τετέλεσται, "perfected," "brought to completion," 19:30)—refers back to Genesis 1:26 is witnessed to, unwittingly, by Pilate: "Behold the human being" (John 19:5). Christ is the reality of which Adam was only a sketch, a type, as Paul had put it, of the one to come (Rom 5:12).

Our interest here, however, is in Genesis 2. If the work on the cross completes the project announced in Genesis 1, Genesis 2 then speaks of how the woman was made from the side of the sleeping Adam, providing John with further imagery for describing the passion: the blood and water flowing from the side of the crucified Christ. This parallel was already noted by Tertullian:

> As Adam was a figure of Christ, Adam's sleep sketched out the death of Christ, who was to sleep a mortal slumber, so that from the wound inflicted on his side might be figured the true mother of the living, the Church. (*An.* 43.10)

Moreover, according to Genesis, the woman built up from the side of the sleeping Adam was called "Eve" (rendered as *zōē*—"life"—in the LXX),[4] for she is "the mother of the living" (Gen 3:20); but, in fact, all her children die! In reverse, the church, the blood and water flowing from the side of the crucified Christ, is the true mother of the living, although it is through their conformity to Christ's death that her children are born into life.[5]

John's playfulness continues even further, with three instances where the "woman" addressed or spoken about by Christ is a mother. First, at the marriage in Cana on the third day, "Woman, what have you to do with me?," with the addition, "My hour is not yet" (John 2:1–4). Second, in Christ's farewell discourse, where the woman is now in travail, having sorrow (not pain!); but when she will be delivered of "the infant" (τὸ παιδίον), Christ

---

3. See Behr, *John the Theologian*, 194–217.

4. That the name "Eve" is rendered as *zōē* means, in turn, that mentions of "life" in the Gospel of John should also be heard in both registers; for instance: "I have come that you might have life/*zōē*" (John 10:10). See Hart, *Woman, the Hour, and the Garden*.

5. See Behr, *John the Theologian*, 214–16; Lieu, "Mother of the Son."

says, she will have joy in that "a human being (ἄνθρωπος) has come into the world" (16:21). And finally, at the cross, where Jesus addresses "the mother" (not "his mother," as it is often rendered) with the words, "Woman, behold your son" (John 19:26). Then, moving once again from Genesis 1 to 2: the identification of Adam as the one who was to work the garden (Gen 2:8) is played upon by John when the risen Christ is thought to be "the gardener" by Mary (John 20:15—another Mary: we will turn to "Mary" shortly). The play here delighted the Syriac poets. For instance, a *madrāshā* of the Syriac Catholic Breviary, puts it this way:

> The Lord of Paradise is risen from the tomb
> And Mary saw him and likened him to the gardener.
> He is the Gardener who planted Paradise
> and encircled it with the sword and the cherub.
> You did well, Mary, to call him "Gardener."[6]

Or, from a paschal hymn from the Church of the East, again in dialogue form:

> "O Gardener, how nice is your garden!
> In it there is a tomb and the bridal chamber inside it.
> The guards are sitting at the tomb
> and the chamber, cherubim surround it."
> "How nice of you, Mary, that you have called me 'Gardener!'"[7]

With this transition from mother to spouse begins the second-part of what Peter Leithart has called the "two-part royal romance" that is the Gospel and Revelation: the first part, the Gospel, presents the bridegroom, the Son born by the woman through his passion on the cross; the second part, Revelation, describes the building up of the bride, the church, in those who witness to their faith with their blood. The narrative begins in the Gospel with a marriage at Cana, on the third day, although Christ's hour had not yet come, and concludes at the end of Revelation with the eschatological marriage feast.[8]

---

6. The *madrāshā* is translated in Brock, "Mary and the Gardener." See also Brock, *Mary and Joseph*, 69–85.

7. Quoted in Mengozzi, "Sureth Version of the East-Syriac Dialogue Poem," 159.

8. See Leithhart, *Revelation 1–11*, esp. 22–23.

Early Christians

The imagery of the church as mother or the virgin mother is pervasive in the early years of Christianity. One of the most extensive reflections is found in *The Shepherd of Hermas*. Early on in the work, Hermas has a vision in which an old woman, "clothed in shining garments and holding a book in her hand," appears to him (Herm. *Vis.* 1.2.1). After a second vision, Hermas has another:

> And a revelation was made to me, brethren, while I slept, by a very beautiful young man, who said to me, "Who do you think that the ancient lady was from whom you received the little book?"
> I said, "The Sibyl."
> "You are wrong," he said, "she is not."
> "Who is she, then?" I said.
> "The Church," he said.
> I said to him, "Why then is she old?"
> "Because," he said, "she was created the first of all things. For this reason she is old; and for her sake the world was established."
> (Herm. *Vis.* 2.4.1)

In a later vision, the old woman shows Hermas a tower being built out of stones specifically prepared for the task. The stones that were cracked, rotten, or the wrong shape were rejected, while the stones that were used fitted together so well that the tower seemed to be built out of one stone. When he asked for an explanation, Hermas was told by the woman: "The tower which you see being built is myself, the church, who have appeared to you both now and formerly" (Herm. *Vis.* 3.3.3).

By the time of the fourth vision, the woman changes appearance: having begun as a old woman, the first of all created things, she now appears as a young, virginal, maiden, "'adorned as if coming forth from the bridal chamber' [Ps 19:5/18:6; Rev 21:2], all in white and with white sandals, veiled to her forehead, and a turban for a head-dress, and her hair was white" (Herm. *Vis.* 4.2.1). The church is at once older than the rest of creation—she is created first of all things, and all things are established for her—but, as the revelation continues, she becomes a pure virgin, for it is as a spotless virgin that Paul says he *will* present his communities to Christ (2 Cor 11:2): this is something to be achieved, something that lies in the future.

The idea that the church preexists the world is also found in the *Second Epistle of Clement*:

> So, then, brethren, if we do the will of God our Father, we shall belong to the first Church, the spiritual one, which was created before the sun and moon.... I do not think that you are ignorant of the fact that the living Church is the body of Christ. For the Scripture says, "God made the human being male and female": the male is Christ, the female is the Church . . . and the apostles say that Church is not just of the present but has existed from the beginning; for she was spiritual, as was our Lord Jesus Christ, but she [or he] was made manifest in the last days so that she [or he] might save us. (2 *Clem.* 14)

Jesus Christ and the church exist from the beginning—indeed, they are the male and female of Genesis 1:27; but it is only at the end, in the last times, that they are revealed or made manifest so that we might be saved.

A more unusual example comes from Clement of Alexandria. Here the Virgin is not only our mother, giving us birth into the life of God, but also the one who supplies nourishment to her infants:

> The Lord Christ, fruit of the Virgin, did not proclaim women's breasts to be blessed, nor did he choose them to give nourishment. But when the loving and philanthropic Father rained down his Word, it became spiritual nourishment for the virtuous. O mysterious marvel! There is one Father of all, there is one Word of all, and the Holy Spirit is one and the same everywhere. There is also one Virgin Mother, whom I love to call the Church. This mother, when alone, had no milk because, alone, she was not a woman: she is virgin and mother simultaneously, a virgin undefiled and a mother full of love. She draws her children to herself and nurses them with holy milk, that is, the Word for infants. She had not milk because the milk was this child, beautiful and familiar, the body of Christ, which nourishes by the word the young brood, which the Lord himself brought forth in the throes of the flesh, which the Lord himself swathed in his precious blood. O amazing birth! (*Paed.* 1.6.41.3–42.2)

The fruit of the Virgin here is Christ—however, not simply as the one to whom she gives birth but as her milk, with which she now nourishes those for whom she is mother. And again there is the suggestion that the church already existed, a virgin waiting to become a mother while yet preserving her virginity.

In the work known as *On the Christ and the Antichrist* attributed to Hippolytus, we have a similar way of speaking, connecting the passion to the flesh received from the Virgin:

> For the Word of God, being fleshless, put on the holy flesh from the holy Virgin, as a Bridegroom a garment, having woven it for himself in the sufferings of the cross, so that having mixed our mortal body with his own power, and having mingled the corruptible into the incorruptible, and the weak with the strong, he might save the perishing human being.
> The web-beam, therefore, is the passion of the Lord upon the cross, and the warp on it is the power of the Holy Spirit,
> and the woof is the holy flesh woven by the Spirit,
> and the thread is the grace which by the love of Christ binds and unites the two in one,
> and the rods are the Word;
> and the workers are the patriarchs and prophets who weave the fair, long, perfect tunic for Christ;
> and the Word passing through these, like the combs, completes through them that which his Father wills. (*Antichr.* 4)

The Word saves the perishing human being by receiving flesh from the Virgin which he himself weaves in the sufferings of the cross, mixing his power with our weakness. The weaving imagery used by Hippolytus is not dissimilar to Irenaeus's image of the mosaic: The words and actions of the patriarchs and prophets, woven together by the Word and the Spirit, upon the beam of the cross, provides the perfect and long tunic of Christ. In this case, Hippolytus later affirms, following Revelation 12, the Virgin is the church, who will never cease "bearing from her heart the Word that is persecuted by the unbelieving in the world," while the male child she bears is Christ, God and human, announced by the prophets, "whom the Church continually bears as she teaches all nations [ὃν ἀεὶ τίκουσα ἡ ἐκκλησία διδάσκει πάντα τὰ ἔθνη]" (*Antichr.* 61).

And then, perhaps with more familiar imagery, Cyprian of Carthage, for whom the church is both the spouse of Christ and our mother:

> She spreads her branches in generous growth over all the earth, she extends her abundant streams ever further; yet one is the head-spring, one the source, one the Mother who is prolific in her offspring, generation after generation; of her womb are we born, of her milk are we fed, from her Spirit our souls draw their life-breath. The spouse of Christ cannot be defiled, she is inviolate and chaste; she knows one home alone, in all modesty she keeps faithfully to one chamber. It is she who seals for the kingdom the sons who she has borne. Whoever breaks with the Church and enters on an adulterous union, cuts himself off from the promises made

to the Church. . . . You cannot have God for your Father if you no longer have the Church for your mother. (*Unit. eccl.*, 5–6)

But it is above all in Irenaeus that we see the imagery deployed most creatively and scripturally. Irenaeus, as noted earlier, was the likely author of the "Letter of the Christians of Vienne and Lyons," which described the virgin mother as rejoicing when those who had previously denied their faith were brought back to the arena by the witness of Blandina and Attalus. Irenaeus's most developed exploration of this theme occurs in the fourth book of *Against the Heresies*, where he gives an account of the ecclesial reading of the scriptures as carried out by true presbyters and spiritual disciples (*Haer.* 4.26.2–33.15).[9] After recounting how a spiritual disciple, on the basis of this reading, can refute various errors and giving a summary statement of this true knowledge, Irenaeus then segues seamlessly into speaking about the church: She is the one who "in every place, because of that love which she cherishes towards God, sends forward throughout all times a multitude of martyrs to the Father"; she is the one who "alone sustains with purity the reproach of those who suffer persecution for righteousness' sake and endure all sorts of punishments and are put to death because of the love which they bear to God and their confession of his Son" (*Haer.* 4.33.9). The persecution of those upon whom the Spirit would rest and who would obey the Word of God was foretold by the prophets, who also prefigured it in their own lives "because of their love of God and on account of his Word." In so doing, however, they not only prefigured Christ but also contributed to the completion of the economy, "in the same way that the activity of the entire body is shown by our members—for the figure of the whole human is not shown by a single member but by all—so also the prophets, while all prefiguring the one [Christ], did each of them, in accordance with their position as a member, complete the economy and foreshadow the work of Christ connected with that member" (*Haer.* 4.33.10).

Irenaeus then continues by giving a tapestry of scriptural quotations and allusions, exemplifying the complete figure witnessed to by the prophets (*Haer.* 4.33.11–14).[10] He begins by alluding to Isaiah, who beheld him in glory at the right hand of the Father (Isa 6:1; cf. Ps 110:1/109:1), while others saw him coming on the clouds (Dan 7:13), and yet others said of

---

9. Following the passage cited in chapter 1 on Christ as the treasure hidden in the scriptures. For this as a distinct section, see Behr, *Irenaeus of Lyons*, 96–97.

10. The first two groups of OT quotations are also followed by words of Christ and Paul.

him, "They shall look on him whom they have pierced" (Zech 12:10), indicating his *parousia*, to which Christ himself referred (when asking whether the Son of Man would find faith when he comes, Luke 18:8) and so, too, Paul (2 Thess 1:6–8). Yet others saw him as a judge, speaking of the fire of the Day of the Lord (Ps 50:6/49:6; Mal 4:1), to which the words of Christ and Paul again bear witness (Matt 3:12; Luke 3:17; Matt 25:41; 2 Thess 1:9–10). The third group of quotations (Ps 45:2, 7, 3–4/44:3, 8, 4–5) speak about that beauty and splendor of his kingdom and "the transcendent and pre-eminent exaltation of all those under his reign." Irenaeus follows this scriptural tapestry with this arresting passage:

> Those, again, saying, "He is a man, and who shall know him?" [Jer 17:9], and, "I came unto the prophetess, and she bore a son, and his name is called Wonderful Counselor, mighty God" [Isa 8:3; 9:6], and who proclaimed the one from the Virgin [to be] Immanuel [cf. Isa 7:14], showed the union of the Word of God with his handiwork, that the Word would become flesh and the Son of God the Son of man—the Pure One opening purely that pure womb which regenerates humans unto God and which he himself made pure—having become that which we are, he is "mighty God" and has a generation which cannot be declared [cf. Isa 53:8 LXX]. (*Haer.* 4.33.11)

After this, Irenaeus turns to a series of texts, demonstrating how the prophets (not, this time, Christ and Paul) spoke of Christ's *parousia* from Judea and from Bethlehem, together with the miracles worked by him (*Haer.* 4.33.11); his entry into Jerusalem, suffering, and death (4.33.12); his resurrection and exaltation (4.33.13); and the new covenant he established (4.33.14). One who is truly spiritual, Irenaeus concludes, will look at all the other points uttered by the prophets in the long exposition of scripture, will point out which particular aspect of the economy is being spoken about, and will also make clear the entire body of the work of the Son of God, always knowing the same God and always acknowledging the same Word of God, the same Spirit of God who was poured out upon human beings in a new way in the last times, and the same human race from the *genesis* of the cosmos until the end, in which those who believe in God and follow his Word receive salvation (*Haer.* 4.33.15).

What is particularly arresting and intriguing about this text is not so much that the scriptural quotations (Jer 17:9; Isa 7:14; 8:3; 9:6) show, for Irenaeus, "the union of the Word of God with his handiwork, that the Word would become flesh and the Son of God the Son of man," but how these predictions are in turn explained by the subclause: "The Pure One opening purely that pure womb which regenerates humans unto God and which he himself made pure" (*purus pure puram aperiens vulvam eam quae regenerat homines in Deum, quam ipse puram fecit*). As an explanatory subclause, it provides the explanation for the preceding clauses, which themselves summarize that about which the verses from scripture speak. The "pure womb which regenerates humans unto God" clearly refers to the church, spoken of a little earlier as the one who, because of her love for God, "sends forward throughout all time a multitude of martyrs to the Father" (*Haer.* 4.33.9; cf. 4.33.4). And so, the opening of the pure womb by the Pure One refers to the passion of Christ, the wounded servant of Isa 53, whose wound has become the locus of birth (Isa 54:1) for those who follow him. This connection, already made by Paul and dramatized in Byzantine liturgical practice, was also illustrated in some medieval "Book of Hours," where the wound of the crucified Christ is graphically depicted as a vulva (Image 14), giving further depth to the connection between birth and death (as we explored in the previous chapter) and also perhaps indicating what it is upon which the Virgin reclines in the standard Byzantine image of the nativity (Image 15).

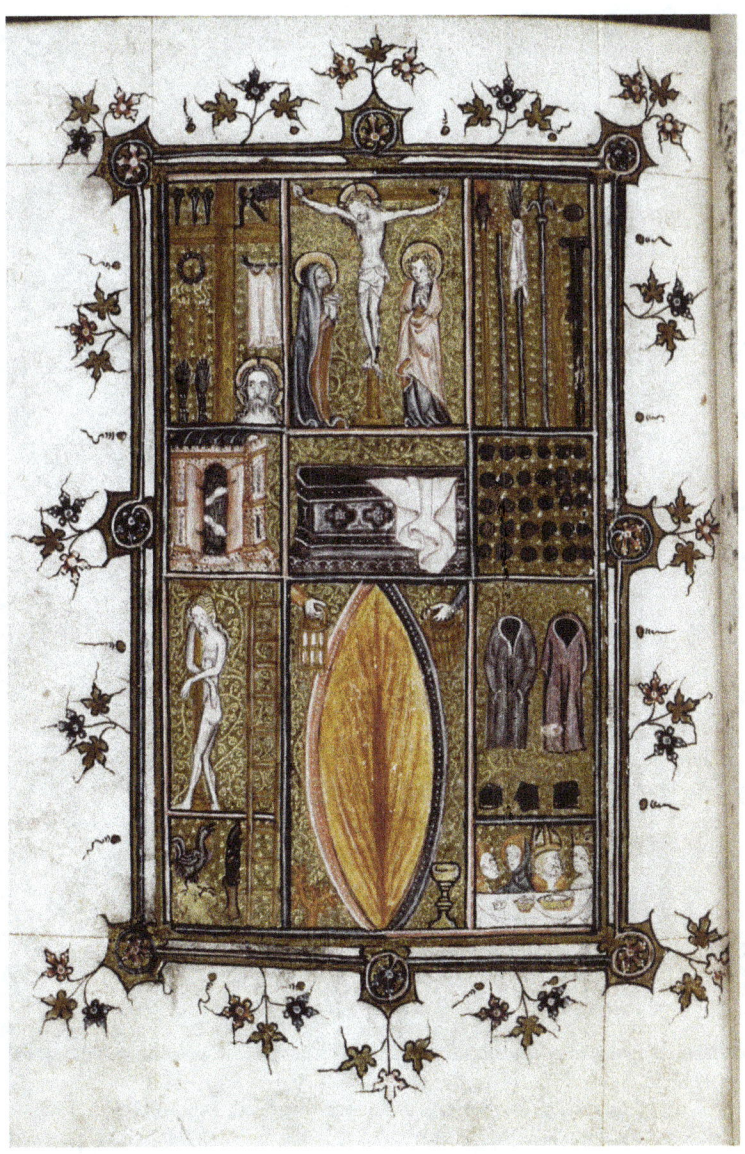

Image 14: The Crucifixion and Wound of Christ, The "Bohun Psalter and Hours," Bodleian Library MS. Auct. D. 4. 4, England, ca. 1370–1380

In Accordance with the Scriptures

Image 15: The Nativity of Christ, Novgorod, 1500–1525

Christ's pascha thus opens the way for our adoption as children of God, born of God (cf. John 1:13) by baptismal conformity to the death of Christ (cf. Rom 5:3–5, etc.), who is "the first-born of many brethren" (Rom 8:29) and is so as "the first-born of the dead" (Col 1:18). Or, as Irenaeus puts it:

> For the Lord, who was born "the first-born of the dead," receiving the ancient fathers into his bosom regenerated them to the life of

80

God, having become the beginning of those who live, as Adam had become the beginning of those who die. (*Haer.* 3.22.4)

It is as "the first-born of the dead" that Christ himself was born from the Virgin, so himself becoming the beginning of life for all those who are regenerated in his own new generation, in the same pure, virginal womb. In other words, Christ's birth from the Virgin cannot be separated from his pascha. Moreover, as our text puts it, it is Christ himself, the Pure One, who not only "opens purely the pure womb," making a path for those who follow him, but in so doing makes that womb "pure." Further, in this way, those who prefigure Christ (and those who figure him now) contribute to the completion of the economy of God, the completion of "the whole human being."

This ancient way of speaking of the church as the Virgin is preserved in the Byzantine hymnography still used in Orthodox worship. For example, the troparion for the resurrection in Tone Six:

> Angelic Powers were at your grave, and those who guarded it became as dead,
> and Mary stood by the tomb, seeking your most pure Body.
> You despoiled Hell and emerged unscathed; you met the Virgin and granted life.
> O Lord, risen from the dead, glory to you![11]

The Virgin, to whom the risen Christ comes, granting life, is the church, now become a virginal mother, granting life to those who are born in her womb through their death in confession of Christ. According to the Gospel accounts, however, it is Mary Magdalene who came to the tomb seeking Christ's body. That here she is spoken of simply as "Mary" introduces us to our next theme: the way in which, with this strong and vivid sense of the church as "virgin mother," Christians began to think of, and speak about, Mary.

Speaking of Mary

Although Paul speaks of the Son having come-to-be from a woman (Gal 4:4), he does not, of course, mention the name "Mary": she appears in the Gospels. After being written about in the Gospels, when Mary begins to appear in early patristic texts, it is usually in terms of her being the New Eve. We find this first in Justin Martyr and then, extensively, in Irenaeus. If Eve

---

11. Translation from Η ΘΕΙΑ ΛΕΙΤΟΥΡΓΙΑ—*The Divine Liturgy*.

had been led astray by a word, it is by receiving the word from the angel that Mary became an advocate for Eve, virginal disobedience being balanced by virginal obedience; and as God formed Adam from virgin earth, so Christ comes from our own virgin earth, to preserve the likeness of formation while maintaining the continuity of earth.[12]

Yet, as we have seen, the prior typology is between Eve and the church, so when Mary is now correlated to Eve, it is overshadowed by the prior figure of the church as virgin mother. Mary's "Magnificat" (Luke 1:46–55) is thus taken by Irenaeus as Mary "prophesying on behalf of the Church" (*Haer.* 3.10.2). From the fourth century onwards, the connection between the church as virgin mother and the virgin mother who is Mary comes to the fore. Ephrem the Syrian, whose poetic writings lend themselves most readily to such associations of images, develops this point extensively. For instance, a propos of the words of those who witnessed the feeding of the five thousand, "This is the prophet who is to come into the world" (John 6:14), Ephrem comments:

> They were repeating that [word] of Moses, "The Lord will raise up a prophet for you," not any ordinary one, but one "like me" [Deut 18:15], who will feed you bread in the desert. "Like me," he walked on the sea [cf. Matt 14:25–31] and appeared in the clouds [cf. Matt 17:5]. He freed his Church from circumcision, and established John, who was a virgin, in place of Joshua, son of Nun. He confided Mary, his Church, to him [cf. John 19:25–27], as Moses [confided] his flock to Joshua [Jesus; cf. Deut. 31:7–8], so that this [word] "like me" might be fulfilled. (*Comm. Diat.* 12.5)

Mary is simply identified as the church. Importantly, this identification is based on the point that they recognize the risen Christ:

> Three angels were seen at the tomb:
> these three announced that he was risen on the third day.
> Mary, who saw him, is the symbol of the Church,
> which will be the first to recognize the signs of his second coming.
> (Ephrem, *Crucifixion* 4.17)[13]

Most striking, however, is a passage attributed to Ephrem, but probably not by Ephrem himself:

---

12. See Justin Martyr, *Dial.* 100; Irenaeus, *Haer.* 3.22.4; 5.19.2; *Dem.* 32–33.

13. See also Ephrem, *Unleavened Bread* 6.6–7, in Gambero, *Mary and the Fathers of the Church*, 115–16; *Nativity* 10.6–8.

The Virgin Mother

> The Virgin Mary is like the Church,
> when she receives the first announcement of the gospel.
> And, as a representative of the Church that Mary sees the risen Jesus.
> Blessed be God, who filled Mary and the Church with joy.
> We call the Church Mary,
> for she deserves both names. (Ps. Ephrem, *Serm.* 7.192–97)[14]

Mary is likened to the church; the church comes first, and Mary is seen as a figure of the church. Moreover, Ephrem passes seamlessly from one Mary to another (from mother to spouse), from the Virgin at the nativity to the one encountering the Risen Lord. That he can do so is due to the specification that Mary, in both cases, is like the church in receiving the gospel.

It is possible that in making this point, the hymn has noticed a striking fact about the Gospel narratives: apart from the infancy narratives and the crucifixion/resurrection accounts, the mother of Jesus is not called Mary but simply "his mother," with one exception, in the question posed by the crowds: "Is this not the carpenter, the son of Mary?" (Mark 6:3; cf. Matt 13:55; the passage is notably absent from Luke, the one whom tradition holds to have painted the first icon of Mary). Indeed, when told that his mother and brother are outside waiting to see him, Jesus asserted "My mother and my brothers are those who hear the word of God and keep it" (Luke 8:21; cf. Matt 12:49–50). Commenting on these words, Chrysostom comments that his mother "wanted to show the people that she had power and authority over her son, imagining not as yet any great thing concerning him." The lesson he draws from this is that "we learn here that even to have borne Christ in the womb, and to have brought forth that marvelous birth, has no profit, if there is not virtue." But, he continues a little later, Christ "has pointed out to us a spacious road: and it is granted not only to women but also to men, to be of this rank, or rather of one yet higher. For this makes one his mother much more than those birth-pangs did" (*Hom. Matt.* 44).[15] On the other hand, no one else is depicted in the Gospels as "hearing the Word and keeping it," apart from Mary: When she receives the first announcement of the gospel, representing the church, the Virgin Mary gives birth to the Christ (the head of the body), and when (the other Mary) encounters the risen Lord, she, too, represents the church, the one who gives birth to the (whole) body of Christ. In both cases, it is the reception of

---

14. For the translation, see Gambero, *Mary and the Fathers of the Church*, 115.
15. PG 57:464–66; cf. Matt 12:46–49.

the gospel that defines "Mary," so Mary is not the archetype of the church, as is sometimes said, but rather the other way round: Theological reflection, beginning already with Paul, began with the figure of the mother, the free Jerusalem above, who, as we have seen, was then held to be created first, older than the world, prefigured in Eve and as Isaiah's barren woman who now gives birth through the passion of Christ, opening purely the pure womb. It is this one to whom "Mary" is likened. While Paul only spoke of the mother of Jesus as "a woman," it is possible that the church, and then his mother, is called "Mary" precisely because it is Miriam/Mary who sang the song of victory after the exodus (Exod 15:21). Irenaeus's assertion that the Magnificat is Mary "prophesying on behalf of the Church" (*Haer.* 3.10.2) is echoed by Raymond Brown, observing that the use of the aorist in the hymn means that

> the Magnificat is vocalizing literally the sentiments of the Jewish Christian Anawim [that is, the poor and afflicted]. The aorists refer to a definite action in the past, namely, the salvation brought about through the death and resurrection of Jesus.... All this praise for what God *had done* could be retroverted and placed on Mary's lips because Luke is interpreting the conception of Jesus in the light not only of the post-resurrectional Christology of the Church, but also of post-resurrectional soteriology, particularly of the Jewish Christian Anawim of Jerusalem as described in Acts.[16]

Again, "Mary" is a figure of the church, as the early Christians saw so clearly.

In the period after Ephrem, from the fifth century onwards, the church and Mary become virtually synonymous, as we can see especially in iconography, hymnography, and in the homilies for the feasts of Mary. For instance, the image of Mary frequently depicted in the apse behind the altar in Byzantine temples—with her arms outstretched in prayer and Christ in a mandorla positioned between her arms—describe her as the one whose womb is wider than the heavens (Πλατυτέρα των Ουρανών; hardly a physiological statement!). The hymnography for her feasts frequently refers to her as the temple, the parts of its architecture (such as the gate that remains closed), its furniture (she is, for instance, the ark of the covenant, in whom the Word of God was contained), or even Jerusalem, as in the paschal hymn to the Theotokos:

---

16. Brown, *Birth of the Messiah*, 363.

Shine Shine O New Jerusalem! The glory of the Lord has shone upon you. Exalt now and be glad, O Zion. Be radiant, O pure Theotokos, in the resurrection of your Son.[17]

Image 16: The Anastasis and Holy Zion, the Chludov Psalter (Historical Museum, Moscow, ms. gr. 129, 100ᵛ), Byzantine, ninth century

In the words of Gregory Palamas, for the feast of her Dormition, "she alone stands at the border between the created and the uncreated nature, and no one can come to God unless he is truly illuminated by her"; she is "an icon of everything good," and "a world of everything good, both visible and invisible."[18]

We have considered the iconographic depiction of the nativity in the prior chapter, noting how it plays upon the paschal theme, rendering it as a birth. Similar points can be made regarding the iconography of the Mother and Child. As Maximos Constas notes:

> The iconography of Mother and Child likewise anticipates the loss of the child to death on the cross. These seemingly simple compositions are in fact saturated with complex allusions to the Passion: the look of sorrow on the mother's face, the child's reclining posture, his bare (left) leg or legs, his legs crossed at the ankle, his raised heal and/or dangling sandal, his golden fluttering garment,

---

17. See the hymnography for the Marian feasts in *Festal Menaion*; cf. Banev, "Myriad of Names," 75–103.

18. Gregory Palamas, *Homily* 37.10, 15.

In Accordance with the Scriptures

and many other signs and symbols make these images compelling anticipations of the child's sacrifice on the cross.[19]

Sometimes, as in the "Amolyntos" icon, with angels bearing the cross and the spear, the focus of the image is made explicit (Image 17).

Image 17: The Icon of the Virgin of the Passion (Amolyntos), Byzantine and Christian Museum, Athens, ca. 1610

19. Constas, *Art of Seeing*, 104.

Image 18: The Virgin Kardiotissa, Angelos Akotantos, 1400–1450

But it is "Kardiotissa" icon (Image 18) that renders the connection between the Christ and his passion most directly, and thereby the identity of the mother: the child's head is turned backwards, as would the head of bird of sacrifice once the neck is broken (cf. Lev 5:8; Luke 2:24), while his arms are outstretched, embracing his mother. Again, as Constas puts it:

In these powerful and perhaps even disturbing images, the child's arms are raised as if on the cross, for the body of the mother is the locus of the divinity's self-emptying, the "region of unlikeness" [Plato, *Statesman* 273d], the matrix in which God assumed the "form of a slave" and became "obedient to the point of death, even death on a cross" [Phil 2:8]. The *Kardiostissa* type is thus a mirror held up to the future, in which, by anticipation, we see Christ crucified in reverse (that is, with his back to the viewer). These icons give graphic expression to the doctrine that the self-emptying of God in the Incarnation signals the death of God; that the incarnation is a voluntary "crucifixion" in which the divinity is nailed to the flesh, the body of the Mother. "I therefore call the Mother of God a cross," said one of the Church Fathers, "for the Lord was suspended on her outstretched arms."[20]

The (single) mystery of Christ's pascha, the cross, is, as we suggested in the last chapter, refracted into a spectrum of feasts and images, each of which is stamped by the form of the cross. As Constas concludes: "Seen from this point of view, the icon of the crucifixion is not simply *another* icon within a series of icons, but rather the matrix from which all icons emerge, the focal point on which their divergent forms converge."[21]

Ecclesiology

It is striking that this maternal imagery of the church, with its deep scriptural roots and grounding in the very proclamation of the gospel, is as pervasive in early Christianity as it is absent in modern ecclesiological reflection. Hugo Rahner gathered together many passages from the first millennium praising the church as "Mater Ecclesia."[22] And Henri de Lubac wrote a study entitled *The Motherhood of the Church*, which briefly touches on the themes we have been discussing, though usually proceeding from the Virgin Mary to the church by analogy.[23] More in line with what we have seen is the brief suggestion of Vladimir Lossky that the hypostasis of the church is to be found in the person of Mary,[24] and one can find similar ideas worked out, in

---

20. Constas, *Art of Seeing*, 104–5, citing Ps. Epiphanios (PG 43:497c).
21. Constas, *Art of Seeing*, 106.
22. Rahner, *Mater Ecclesia*.
23. Lubac, *Motherhood of the Church*.
24. Lossky, *Mystical Theology*, 193.

The Virgin Mother

a different manner, in the Sophiology of Sergius Bulgakov.[25] None of these, however, seem to have impacted contemporary ecclesiology in any significant manner. And so, to conclude this chapter, we should consider what contribution would be made by thinking again of the church, beginning not with institutions and their structures but with this maternal dimension.

There are two points that are worth reflecting upon. The first concerns the sacraments of baptism and eucharist and, bound up with this, the "royal priesthood" of believers (1 Pet 2:9). When James and John approach Jesus to ask to sit at his right and left hand when he comes into his glory, Jesus asks them: "Are you able to drink the cup that I drink, or to be baptized with the baptism with which I am baptized?" (Mark 10:38). As we have seen, our entry into the paschal mystery of Christ is through our voluntary, martyric death, following Christ, to be born into the life of the resurrection. This is what it is to drink the cup and be baptized. That this is so for baptism is clear; it is indicated by the significant change of tense in the apostle's statement: "If we *have been* united within him in a death like his, we *shall certainly be united* with him in a resurrection like his" (Rom 6:5). The reason for this change of tense from past to future is simply the fact that we are not yet dead! And so Paul urges us: "Consider yourself dead to sin and alive to God in Christ Jesus" (Rom 6:11). The same point can be made regarding the eucharist: The invitation to share in the cup is an invitation to share in his passion. One can, perhaps, go even further. When Ignatius wrote to the Christians in Rome, urging them not to interfere with his impending fate, he saw his martyrdom as his becoming the very eucharistic gifts: "I am God's wheat and through the beasts' teeth I shall be found to be the pure bread for Christ" (Ign. *Rom.* 4.1). One can see same point in the Martyrdom of Polycarp: When his body was finally put to the flames, those around him smelled baking bread (*Mart. Pol.* 15.2).[26] We will see Irenaeus develop this imagery further in the next chapter. As such, when Ignatius describes the eucharist as being "the medicine of immortality" (Ign. *Eph.* 20.2), he is not saying that if we partake as often as possible we will not die but rather that by sharing in the cup, in the fullness of what that means, we are *already* partaking of the life that comes through death and so cannot be touched by death. The sacraments of baptism and eucharist are thus anticipations of each person's own entry into Christ's paschal mystery through their actual death and resurrection. It is this that marks believers as a "royal

---

25. See Louth, "Mary the Mother of God and Ecclesiology."
26. See Johnson, "Martyrs and the Mass."

priesthood," as those who, in their own actual death (anticipated in baptism and taking up the cross to live for others not themselves), are the ones who are making the offering, which they themselves are (as Christ is "the one who offers and is offered"), and so each—whether male or female, lay or ordained—is *the* priest of their entry into Christ's paschal mystery, finally at their death and anticipating this in the course of their lives.

The Spirit given in the seal of the sacrament of baptism is, as Paul puts it, "the pledge [ἀρραβών, or 'guarantee'] of our inheritance until we acquire possession of it" (Eph 1:13). Even now, Irenaeus says, the pledge "tends towards perfection, preparing us for incorruption." But what shall it be like when the complete grace is given, he asks: "It will render us like unto him and accomplish the will of the Father, making the human being in the image and likeness of God" (*Haer.* 5.8.1). It is, moreover, as Irenaeus puts it, "a gift of God, entrusted to the church, as the breath was to the first created human being," so that "where the Church is, there is the Spirit of God, and where the Spirit of God is, there is the Church" (*Haer.* 3.24.1). If, then, as the Psalmist addresses God, "you take away their breath, they die and return to the dust, you send forth your Spirit and they will be created and you renew the face of the earth" (Ps 104:29–30/103:29–30), we can perhaps go further to say that the church—the *ekklesia* that is embodied, manifest, realized in each local community—is not simply a community of those called out *from* the world into yet another grouping in the world alongside many other bodies but rather those who are called out *into* the life of the new creation, the eighth day, and are already anticipating that eschatological reality. These ecclesial communities are, as it were, the signs of the new life that comes through death, as fresh grass and crocuses appearing in winter, amidst the deadened world, herald the springtime of the renewed earth. Which, in turn, or in reverse, means that the church is really the whole of creation seen eschatologically, for the church is not only our mother but also the bride of Christ, being prepared for the eschatological marriage to become one with Christ, and thus the church is also the body of Christ, when all things have been brought into subjection to him, as the head of the body, so that he, in turn, can subject all things to God, and so God will be all in all (1 Cor 15:28).

The second point concerns organization. If the church is our heavenly virgin mother, in whose womb we enter into the paschal mystery of Christ, an entry that is anticipated in the sacraments of baptism and eucharist and realized in our own priestly life, death, and resurrection, the church is nevertheless instantiated in particular local communities where the life of the kingdom is already beginning to be lived. What, then, can we say about the relationship between these particular local communities?

As the number of Christians grew and there were more than one ecclesial body in a given place, it became necessary to coordinate the activity of these different communities. We see this happening first in big cities such as Rome and Alexandria.[27] Already before Paul arrived in Rome, there were a number of different Christian communities in existence there (cf. Rom 16). In Antioch, Ignatius speaks of the bishop, the presbyters, the deacon, and all the people gathered together comprising the body of the church; though he is referring to a single community—a house church—not a diocese composed of many parishes headed by a bishop. In Rome, on the other hand, there were a number of communities alongside each other, and the leader of each community was known as both bishop and presbyter, even as late as the time of Irenaeus: as the head of his own community, he was the bishop, the overseer, but when gathered together with leaders of other communities, as we can see from Hermas, these figures were referred to as presbyters—"elders"—constituting together a college. How they related to each other was, inevitably, difficult and fraught. Hermas describes how there was jostling among the leaders for the "first seats" or for "privileges and reputation" (Herm. *Vis.* 3.9.7; Herm. *Sim.* 8.7.4-6)—nothing changes! It was only by the end of the second century (or even early in the third) that this federated system coalesced into a single body under a single head, for whom the term "bishop" was now reserved, with the term "presbyter" now being used for the leaders of the various communities under the bishop's oversight. This change is also evident in the practice of the fermentum: whereas originally each community shared its eucharist gifts with all the other communities, it now became exclusively the bishop's eucharistic gifts that were distributed to his presbyters leading the different parishes.[28] Over time, this coordination was extended beyond the cities into a system of dioceses headed by a bishop, comprised of parishes headed by the bishop's priests, and then, in due time, ever greater areas, archdioceses, patriarchates, and so on, into today's national "churches."

It was and is necessary, of course, to coordinate the various local ecclesial communities. But the word "church" is not the appropriate term for this

---

27. See especially Stewart, *Original Bishops*. For Rome, see Lampe, *From Paul to Valentinus*, and, more briefly, Behr, *Irenaeus of Lyons*, 21–57.

28. See Behr, *John the Theologian*, 80–81; cf. *Hist. Eccl.* 5.24.14–17.

institutional coordination—as if there can be national "churches" when in Christ there is neither Jew nor Greek. Interestingly, this point is reflected in the language of the Orthodox Liturgy: In the course of celebrating the Liturgy, the bishop is primarily spoken of as being the "archpriest," for it is his priestly ministry that is exercised in the liturgy; his "episcopal" work as overseer or administrator, holding together the various communities under his oversight, is an administrative function. In the Liturgy of St. John Chrysostom, the congregation prays for the bishop that he "may serve your holy churches in peace": the word "church" is used for each of the communities that he oversees; the diocese for which he has the administrative role of oversight (*episkopē*) is not a church. To put it the other way round, the bishop, in this administrative role, might well be (and should be!) for the *bene esse* of the churches, but the bishop is not of the *esse* of the church.

Words are, however, slippery, and the word "church" has been used in many ways over the centuries. But we should be careful in our usage, lest we end up transferring to one thing what really belongs to another, for instance, by speaking of the church of Rome or Constantinople or Canterbury as the "mother church," transferring to a particular see what really belongs to the heavenly mother. Similarly, much modern ecclesiology is given over to questions, which do indeed need to be dealt with, of organization, hierarchy, and territory, just as how, in the earliest period, the way the different communities were to relate needed to be established. And just as in the early period this was difficult and often resulted in splits, so, too, in modern times. But from what we have seen of the earliest ways of talking about the church, hopefully a bigger and broader vision of the church has opened up: the church as our heavenly mother in whose womb we are born into life by taking up the cross, manifesting already now the resurrectional life that is to come, a life that can't be touched by death because it has been entered into through death; a life, moreover, that is the first flowering of the new creation.

4

Becoming Human

THE SHAPE OF CHRISTIAN theology, as we have argued in the previous chapters, has come to be determined by the shape of scripture as we now know it—"The Bible." It begins with the creation of the world and Adam and Eve, in a primordially perfect state, who then fall into the state of mortality, bringing death into the world, and then the long history of salvation, culminating in the conception and birth of Jesus, his ministry, and then his crucifixion, resurrection, ascension, and the sending of the Spirit, initiating the mission of the church to spread the gospel. Within this framework, the question inevitably arose whether "the incarnation" was occasioned by the "fall" (as a Plan B) or would have happened anyway. But as we have seen, it is only in the light of the end that we can even begin to understand the beginning, and, moreover, when the scriptures are read in this way, the sacrifice upon the cross is not simply understood as the satisfaction or remedy for sin but rather as an act of love that opens up the womb for us to be born into life by following "the pioneer of our salvation" (Heb 2:10), "the first-born of the dead" (Col 1:18; Rev 1:5), "the first-born of many brethren" (Rom 8:29), and indeed the "beginning" of God's creation (Rev 3:14). The arc of the economy of God is not simply from a "fall" to salvation but from creation to the eschaton, within which sin and death are but a smaller arc or sub-theme: the arc of the single economy proceeds from the type to the reality, from the sketch that is Adam to the fullness of humanity manifest in Christ. To see more fully how this single economy is understood, we will turn to Irenaeus of Lyons, Gregory of Nyssa, and Maximos the Confessor.

Irenaeus of Lyons

Irenaeus interprets the description of Adam as a "type" (Rom 5:14) by reference to the transition Paul sketches in 1 Corinthians 15:45–49.[1] Adam "is a type of the one to come," he says,

> because the Word, the Fashioner of all things, prefigured in him the future economy relating to the Son of God on behalf of the human race, God having predetermined the first, the animated human that is, so that he should be saved by the spiritual [one]; for, since the Savior pre-exists, it was necessary that the one to be saved should also exist, so that the Savior should not be without purpose. (*Haer.* 3.22.3)

The starting point for understanding the economy is the Savior: Since he exists, it is necessary that the one to be saved should also exist. One must start with Christ, not Adam, for the existence of a type presumes that of the prototype or archetype. But the type is now seen not to be the reality itself but a starting point, and the progression from one to the other, following Paul, is from an animated existence to a spiritual one. As Irenaeus puts it in a passage we have already seen, but now can be appreciated anew:

> Just as, at the beginning of our formation in Adam, the breath of life from God, having been united to the handiwork, animated [*animavit*] the human being and showed him to be a rational being, so also, at the end, the Word of the Father and the Spirit of God, having become united with the ancient substance of the formation of Adam, rendered the human being living [*viventem*] and perfect, bearing the perfect Father, in order that just as in the animated we all die, so also in the spiritual we may all be vivified. For never at any time did Adam escape the Hands of God, to whom the Father speaking, said, "Let us make the human being in our image, after our likeness" [Gen 1:26]. And for this reason at the end, "not by the will of the flesh, nor by the will of man" [John 1:13], but by the good pleasure of the Father, his Hands perfected a living human being [*vivum perfecerunt hominem*], in order that Adam might become in the image and likeness of God. (*Haer.* 5.1.3)

The arc of the economy leads from type to reality, from Adam to Christ, from breath to Spirit, and it does so, as it does for Paul, specifically through death and resurrection. It is, thereby, fully eschatologically oriented: It is at the end that Adam, the creature from the earth (both individually and

---

1. For a full exposition of the themes sketched here, see Behr, *Irenaeus of Lyons*.

collectively), comes to be in the image and likeness of God. The completion of the project of God, to make a human being in his image and likeness, refers not to protology but eschatology. It is, moreover, a process that is continuous throughout all time: never does Adam escape the Hands of God.

Having just come into existence, Adam and Eve are, for Irenaeus, but infants, inexperienced in virtue and needing to grow.[2] Moreover, as it had only been "said" that the human was created in the image of God, but not "shown," Adam, not seeing the image, by grasping the fruit of the tree, lost any resemblance to God, falling under the power of the deceiver; while Christ, as the fully grown human, not counting equality with God a thing to be grasped but voluntarily being nailed to the tree, shows us the image of God, and so reestablished the likeness by "assimilating the human being to the invisible Father through the means of the visible Word" (*Haer.* 5.16.2–3; cf. Phil 2:6). In this way, the economy of God on behalf of the human race is already prefigured in Adam, with the end reversing the beginning, so that Christ's death becomes the means of birth into life.

The arc of the economy from Adam to Christ is thus a process of growth, from infancy to maturity. Indeed, having been created, the human being is instructed to grow: God "formed the human being for growth and increase, as the Scripture says, 'increase and grow'" (*Haer.* 4.11.1; Gen 1:28). But growth requires time, which further entails death, for as he notes, "everything that has a beginning in time must also have an end in time" (*Haer.* 4.4.1). And this applies to creation as a whole, though with a nuance: "The fashion of the whole world," he says, "will pass away when the time of its disappearance has come," and yet some things within the world are temporal for the sake of the fruit that they produce, so the wheat can be gathered into the barn while the chaff left behind (*Haer.* 4.4.3). The human being, however, he continues, endowed with reason and free will, sometimes becomes wheat and sometimes chaff. And so, Irenaeus concludes, "God, who is one and the same, who rolls up the heaven as a book and renews the face of the earth, made the things of time for the human, so that, coming to maturity in them, he may produce the fruit of immortality" (*Haer.* 4.5.1). The time of the world, or our time in the world, is the time of our growth towards the end, which has been set from the beginning.

The arc of the economy is described in various ways by Irenaeus. For instance, he speaks of the human being becoming "harmonized to the symphony of salvation" (*Haer.* 4.14.2) or, alternatively, of God and the human

---

2. See Steenberg, "Children in Paradise."

being becoming "accustomed" to each other, with the Spirit gradually becoming accustomed to dwell in human beings, first sporadically and ecstatically in the prophets, but then coming to rest permanently upon Jesus Christ, who then bestows the Spirit upon those who follow him (who stand at the foot of the cross, cf. John 19:3), initially in the form of a "pledge" (2 Cor 1:22; Eph 1:14), accustoming them, until the point that the Spirit is poured out upon all flesh.[3] This accustoming culminates, for Irenaeus, in the witness of the martyrs, who bear their witness not in the frailty of the flesh but rather in the strength of the Spirit. As Irenaeus puts it,

> When the weakness of the flesh is absorbed, it manifests the Spirit as powerful; and again, when the Spirit absorbs the weakness, it inherits the flesh for itself, and from both of these is made a living human being: living, indeed, because of the participation of the Spirit; and human, because of the substance of the flesh. (*Haer.* 5.9.2; cf. Matt 26:41)

The "living human being" that is "the glory of God" is specifically the martyr (*Haer.* 4.20.7).

The most interesting and extended treatment Irenaeus gives of this process of growth is in the concluding chapters of the fourth book of *Against the Heresies*. Here he addresses his opponents' question (or rather complaint) as to why it was that God did not make us perfect from the beginning but rather created us to grow towards perfection, and, even more troubling, why it was that God created humans with freedom and discernment, so "they immediately became ungrateful" towards God, rather than making them like irrational animals, who only have "one inclination and one bearing, unable to deviate and without the power of judgement, and so unable to be anything other than what they were created" (*Haer.* 4.37.6). But to be other than how one has come into being—to be a mature human rather than an infant—requires growth, which as we have seen requires time. Irenaeus countered his opponents' argument by pointing out that not having the possibility of growth, and the struggle it entails, would have benefitted neither God nor us: communion with God would not be something to strive after and, without that striving, neither precious nor even desired. So it is that both Christ and Paul emphasized the need for struggle to grow in our love of God (*Haer.* 4.37.7; citing Matt 11:12; 1 Cor 9:24–27). Moreover, by way of analogy, Irenaeus points out that the faculty of sight is

---

3. See *Haer.* 3.17.1; 3.20.2; 3.35.1; 4.5.4; 4.14.2; 4.21.3; 5.5.1; 5.8.1; Évieux, "La Théologie."

valued more by those who know what it is to be without sight and likewise health by the contrast with sickness, light by darkness, and life by death (*Haer.* 4.37.7; cf. 3.20.1–2). He then concludes this part of his argument:

> The Lord has therefore borne all these things on our behalf, in order that we, having been instructed by means of them all, may be in all respects circumspect for the time to come, and that, having been rationally taught to love God, we may continue in his perfect love: for God has displayed long-suffering in the case of human apostasy, while the human being has been instructed by it, as also the prophet says, "Your own apostasy shall instruct you" [Jer 2:19]. God thus determining all things beforehand for the perfection of the human being, and towards the realization and manifestation of his economies, that goodness may be displayed and righteousness accomplished, and so that the Church may be "conformed to the image of his Son" [Rom 8:29], and so that, finally, the human being may brought to such maturity as to see and comprehend God. (*Haer.* 4.37.7)

To use Irenaeus's imagery of Adam and Eve as children, newborn infants, unlike other animals, do not walk immediately after birth but only after a period of exercising, intrinsic to which is falling down and getting up again. While this no doubt pains the parent as well as the infant, the parent bears with this falling down, knowing the good that will ultimately come about through it. Thus, for Irenaeus, human disobedience, apostasy, and even death itself is inscribed into the very unfolding of the economy (which, we must remember, is always told from the perspective of the end). That which comes into being will no doubt pass away, but this passage, now seen in the light of Christ, is a passage into life rather than mortal animation. Yet it is something towards which we must grow; indeed, it takes a lifetime to learn how to die. This end, moreover, displays the goodness of God and accomplishes his righteousness. And although worked out in and through the life of each human being, the end result is nevertheless corporate: it is the church that is conformed to the image of the Son so that the human being can finally be brought to maturity in seeing and comprehending God.

A few chapters later, Irenaeus presents a similar analysis through the contrast between two types of knowledge: that gained through hearsay and that gained through experience (*Haer.* 4.39.1). There are, he notes, certain things that can only be learnt through experience, such as bitterness and sweetness, and likewise, he claims, it is only through the experience of both good and evil, the latter being disobedience and death, that we receive the knowledge of the good, that is, obedience to God, and so reject the evil through repentance and become ever more tenacious in our obedience to God, thereby growing into maturity and the fullness of life. The alternative, he dramatically says, is that "if anyone shuns the knowledge of both of these, and the twofold perception of knowledge, forgetting himself he destroys the human being" (*Haer.* 4.39.1).

The intervening chapter lays out the full scope and stages of the economy. Here, Irenaeus suggests that God could indeed have created the human being perfect or as a "God" from the beginning, for all things are possible to him. But, as newly created, the human being is initially "infantile," and so "unaccustomed to and unexercised in perfect conduct" (*Haer.* 4.38.1). As a mother could certainly give solid food to a newborn infant, but it wouldn't benefit the infant, "so also," Irenaeus continues, "it was possible for God himself to have made the human being perfect from the first, but the human being could not receive this, being as yet an infant" (*Haer.* 4.38.1). What is needed, again, is growth, a process of accustoming the human being to bear the life and glory of God. And here we return to the issue he identified in his opponents' position: that without freedom and the possibility for growth, the creature would never be able to become something more than it was at first. By definition, of course, the created cannot be uncreated, but this is not a restriction upon the omnipotence of God, for this omnipotence is demonstrated, for Irenaeus, in the way that the created *is* in fact brought *in time* to share in the uncreated life of God, a change in the "fashion" of its existence or the mode of its life, which requires preparation and training, and it is to this end that the whole economy has aimed and been tending. He then continues by explaining how the economy demonstrates God's power, wisdom, and goodness:

> With God power, wisdom, and goodness are demonstrated simultaneously: power and goodness in that he willingly created and made things previously not existing; wisdom in having made those things that have come into being rhythmical and harmonious and elaborate [εὔρυθμα καὶ ἐμμελῆ καὶ ἐγκατάσκευα], which, through the superabundance of his goodness, receiving growth and continuing for a long period, obtain the glory of the Uncreated [ἀγενήτου δόξαν ἀποίσεται], of the God who ungrudgingly bestows good. By virtue of being created, they are not uncreated; but by virtue of continuing in being throughout a long course of ages, they shall receive the power of the Uncreated [δύναμιν ἀγέννητου

προσλήψεται], of the God who freely bestows upon them eternal existence. (*Haer.* 4.38.3)

He continues by describing the different roles: with the Father planning and commanding, the Son executing and performing, and the Spirit giving nourishment and growth, the human being "makes progress day by day, ascending to perfection, that is, approaching the Uncreated One" (*Haer.* 4.38.3). He then enumerates the stages involved:

> It was first necessary for the human being to be created;
> and having been created, to increase;
> and having increased, to become an adult;
> and having become an adult, to multiply;
> and having multiplied, to become strong;
> and having been strengthened, to be glorified;
> and being glorified, to see his Master. (*Haer.* 4.38.3)

What is most striking about this description of the stages of the economy—the growth of the human being from Adam to Christ—is that it is patterned upon the life of each human being, the "seven stages" of life, a pattern of reflection going back to Hippocrates. This sevenfold pattern of human growth also holds for Jesus, according to a tradition probably going back to the evangelist John. Elsewhere, Irenaeus reports that the elders (Papias is certainly the source) who conversed with John in Asia related how Jesus recapitulated all the stages of human life in himself becoming an infant, a child, boy, youth, and, indeed, an old man—for in the Gospel of John (8:57) Jesus is asked: "You are not yet fifty and yet you have seen Abraham," something, Irenaeus points out, one would only ask of someone past forty (*Haer.* 2.22.4).[4] This tradition is paralleled in a passage by Victorinus of Pettau, and thus independently of Irenaeus, stating that Christ "consummates his humanity [*humanitatem . . . consummat*] in the number seven: birth, infancy, boyhood, youth, young-manhood, maturity, death."[5] Τετέλεσται—it is finished, completed, perfected.

Those, then, "who await not the time of increase, but ascribe to God the infirmity of their nature" are truly irrational and ungrateful, Irenaeus concludes, unwilling to be what they have been created at the outset, but wishing to be like God even before they have learnt to become human. The truth of both sides of the human condition is, for Irenaeus, expressed

---

4. The five ages here would increase to seven when one includes birth and death. See Chapman, "Papias on the Age of Our Lord."

5. Victorinus of Pettau, *On the Making of the World*, 9.

in verses from the Psalms: "I have said, you are Gods, all sons of the Most High, but you will die like human beings" (*Haer.* 4.38.4; Ps 82:6–7/81:6–7). Irenaeus concludes his analysis in *Haer.* 4.37–39 by exhorting patience:

> How then will you be a God, when you are not yet made human? How perfect, when only recently begun? How immortal, when in mortal nature you did not obey the Creator? It is necessary for you first to hold the rank of human, and then to participate in the glory of God. For you do not create God, but God creates you. If, then, you are the work of God, await the Hand of God, who does everything at the appropriate time, the appropriate time for you, who are being made. Offer to him your heart, soft and pliable, and retain the shape with which the Fashioner shaped you, having in yourself his Water, lest you turn dry and lose the imprint of his fingers. By guarding this conformation, you will ascend to perfection; the mud in you will be concealed by the art of God. His Hand created your substance; it will gild you, inside and out, with pure gold and silver, and so adorn you that the King himself will desire your beauty. (*Haer.* 4.39.2)

If the arc of the economy as a whole, from the infant Adam to the mature Christ, is patterned upon the life-span of each human being, then the life-span of each human being can, in turn, be seen as recapitulating the same economy. And so we find a fuller vision of what we noted in the first chapter, that the "time" of scripture (cf. Figure 7 in chapter 1) is the time it takes us to read, repeatedly, but each time with a deeper understanding of the mystery of Christ, as we grow from Adam to Christ, from our *genesis* to our *gennēsis*, a growth that requires time—and patience—as we learn to share in the power of the Uncreated.

One further and striking way in which Irenaeus sketches out the whole economy is through an analogy with the eucharist:

> Just as the wood of the vine, planted in the earth, bore fruit in its own time, and the grain of wheat, falling into the earth and being decomposed, was raised up manifold by the Spirit of God who sustains all, then, by wisdom, they come to the use of human beings, and receiving the Word of God, become eucharist, which is the Body and Blood of Christ; so also, our bodies, nourished by it, having been placed in the earth and decomposing in it, shall rise in their time, when the Word of God bestows on them the resurrection to the glory of God the Father, who secures immortality for the mortal and bountifully bestows incorruptibility on the corruptible [cf. 1 Cor 15:53], because the power of God is made

perfect in weakness [cf. 2 Cor 12:9], in order that we may never become puffed up, as if we had life from ourselves, nor exalted against God, entertaining ungrateful thoughts, but learning by experience that it is from his excellence, and not from our own nature, that we have eternal continuance, so that we should neither undervalue the true glory of God nor be ignorant of our own nature, but should know what God can do and what benefits the human, and so that we should never mistake the true understanding of things as they are, that is, of God and the human being. (*Haer.* 5.2.3)

The whole economy, culminating in our death and resurrection, can thus be seen as the eucharist of God, in and through which we learn the truth about God and the human being, "the true understanding of things as they are," that is, reality.

Gregory of Nyssa

Gregory of Nyssa provides us with a further way of conceptualizing the economy of God as the growth of the human being. In his treatise *On the Human Image of God* (otherwise known as *On the Making of Man*), taking Plato's *Timaeus* as a model, Gregory coordinates three analyses.[6] Gregory begins by painting a beautiful picture of the human being as the culmination of creation and, more than that, the image of God. Gregory reads the first chapter of Genesis as an "anthropogony," in which Moses describes the evolution of the soul from its initial power of growth and nutrition evident in plants, then acquiring the power of sense-perception in irrational animals, and culminating in the human being. In this way, as he puts it, "nature makes an ascent, as it were by steps, I mean the properties of life, from the lower to the perfect" (*De hom.* 8.4–7). He emphasizes that the human body is perfectly adapted for the intellect, which God did not so much give to the human being but rather "gave a share in" (*De hom.* 9.1). The human body is upright rather than bent downwards, so it can gaze upon God. It has specially formed hands so that the mouth is free to articulate

---

6. *Timaeus* first presents the "things crafted by Intellect" (47e4), but then points out that the world is in fact of mixed birth, so he must also "give an account of necessity" or "the straying cause" (48a2–3). He then brings these two accounts together under "a final head" (69a7–b12), describing in medical or anatomical terms the constitution of the human being. For a full analysis of Gregory's text and its relation to the *Timaeus*, see the introduction to Behr, *Gregory of Nyssa*.

speech and thereby communicate with others; otherwise, the grace of the intellect would be isolated and incommunicable (*De hom.* 9.1). Moreover, it is as such that we "become rational" (*De hom.* 10.1) through the body, for it is only through the bodily senses that we communicate and learn; the intellect is dependent upon the body for its growth. Gregory also emphasizes that it is in the free exercise of virtue that the human is the living image of the King (*De hom.* 4–5), exercising its sovereignty, as the weakest of all animals, through the cooperation of its subjects (*De hom.* 7). But who this human being is, Gregory does not say.

In the second part of his treatise (*De hom.* 16–29), Gregory takes up the text of Genesis again, asking the question: Where, in fact, do we see such a human being? What we see, empirically, is the pitiable wretchedness of human beings, subject to passion and corruption. And yet scripture does not lie when it says that the human being was made in the image of God. This leads him into a lengthy discussion, full of digressions and changes of voice, analyzing the text of Genesis 1, focusing on: Who the human being spoken of there in fact is; God's prevision of the waywardness of the human will and the need of time for growth; and God's provision for this waywardness. One of the key points in his analysis is that there is a subtle shift between the second and third clause of Genesis 1:27:

> So God made the human in his own image [1:27a]
> in the image of God he made him [1:27b]
> male and female he made them. [1:27c][7]

> "God made," it says, "the human being, in accordance with the image of God he made it." The creation of that which came to be "in accordance with the image" has an end; then it makes a repetition of the account of the formation, and says, "male and female he made them." I think it is known to everyone that this is understood to be outside the Prototype, "for in Christ Jesus," as the apostle says, "there is neither male nor female" [Gal 3:28], but the account says that the human being is indeed divided into these. Therefore the formation of our nature is in a sense twofold, that being likened to the divine, [and] that being divided according to this difference; for something like this the account hints at by the arrangement of what is written, first saying, "God made the human being, in accordance with the image of God he made it,"

7. καὶ ἐποίησεν ὁ θεὸς τὸν ἄνθρωπον
  κατ' εἰκόνα θεοῦ ἐποίησεν αὐτόν
  ἄρσεν καὶ θῆλυ ἐποίησεν αὐτούς

and then, adding to what has been said, "male and female made he them," something that is foreign to our conceptions of God. (*De hom.* 16.7–8)

It is important to note that while each clause of Genesis 1:27 uses the word "made" (ἐποίησεν), Gregory here expounds what is "made" with different words, for as he argues in his *Hexameron*, a companion piece to this treatise, God's act of "making" is instantaneous, encompassing all that is to be, while everything that comes to be is "manifested" in proper order and sequence (*Hex.* 64). So Gregory takes Genesis 1:27ab as indicating that "the creation [κτίσις] of that which has come to be in accordance with the image has an end [τέλος]." That is, it is not that the creation of the human being has been completed but rather that it has an end, a goal, towards which it is oriented, and this, as he puts it in the next sentence, is its Prototype, Christ Jesus. Christ is the *archē* (the beginning, head, source), not Adam, who in fact has not yet been mentioned either by Genesis or by Gregory. Gregory then takes v. 27c ("male and female he made them") as being a "repetition of the account of the formation [κατασκευή]": It is not that God's act of making the human being takes place in two separate stages, as it is often argued, but rather that as v. 27c is a "repetition" of the account of the forming of the human being, it retells the same action but in a slightly different key, indicating that it is the human being (not God's action) that is "two-fold."

This "two-foldedness" of the human formation is then spelled out in the next section:

> I think that by these words Holy Scripture conveys to us a great and lofty doctrine; and the doctrine is this. While two [elements]— the divine and incorporeal nature, and the irrational and animal life—are separated from each other as extremes, the human is the span [μέσον]. For there is to be beheld in the human compound a share of each of those mentioned—of the divine, the rational and intelligent, which does not admit the difference of male and female; of the irrational, the bodily formation and construction, divided into male and female—for each of them is certainly in all that partakes of human life. But the intellectual takes precedence, as we have learnt from one who gives in detail an ordered account of the origin of the human being, participation and kinship with the irrational is concomitant to being human, for he first says that "God made the human being in accordance with the image" of God, showing by what was said, just as the Apostle says, that in such a one "there is not male and female," then he adds the

particularities of human nature, that "male and female he made them." (*De hom.* 16.9)

The human being embraces both the divine and the animal, the rational, and the irrational; these are presented by Moses in an ordered sequence, showing, through the two clauses, that one takes precedence over the other.

As Gregory continues to spell out the difference between the two extremes to show how the divine archetype and the human image differ, it is striking that he does not resort to the human particularities of being male and female. It is, rather, the mutability of human beings that is the issue: the very fact that they have come to be from nothing means that movement, and thus change, lie at the very heart of their existence. It is then on the basis of this mutability that he can answer the problem posed at the beginning of the chapter, and he does so by appealing to the wavering, mutable will of human beings (the equivalent of Timaeus's "straying cause"), the prevision of God regarding this, and his provision for human waywardness. He claims:

> Since, then, the one always remains as it is, while the other, having come into being though creation, began to exist from alteration and has kinship with such change, on this account "he who knows all things before their *genesis*," as the prophecy says [Sus (Θ) 42], following, or rather knowing beforehand, by his power of foreknowledge towards what the movement of human choice inclines, in accordance with its independence and self-determination—since he knows what is to be, he devised for the image the difference according to male and female, which no longer looks to the divine archetype but, as was said, assimilates to the less rational nature. (*De hom.* 16.14)

The argument here seems to be rather circular: This assimilation to the irrational animals is a provision made in foresight of human waywardness, yet it is only because we are already both that we can assimilate ourselves to the irrational. In the next lines, however, he says that he is not stating directly what comes to his mind but instead writing in the form of an exercise for his readers (*De hom.* 16.15). But what is most intriguing in this account is that it is not just a response to why we don't in the present see, immediately or empirically, the image of God in human beings, but that it is given as an explanation for what he has just established as the scriptural account of the two-fold structure of human beings, intellectual and corporeal, with "the particularities of human nature" being existence as male and female. That is, if God's stated purpose in Genesis 1:27 is to make a human being in the image of God, and if, in the Prototype, there is neither male nor female (Gal 3:28), why and for what purpose did God *also* make the human being male and female? That God has done so is not in question, the issue is why he has done so.

Gregory then adds one further element regarding the human being "made" in the image of God in Genesis 1:27a:

> When the account says that "God made the human being," all humankind is indicated by the indefinite character of the term; for the creature was not here also called "Adam," as the narrative that follows relates, but the name given to the created human is not the particular but of the universal. Thus, we are led by the universal name of the nature to suppose something such as this that, by divine foreknowledge and power, all humanity is included in the first formation. For it is fitting for God not to think of any of the things that had come to be by him as indeterminate, but that for each being there should be some limit and measure marked out by the wisdom of the Maker. Now just as any particular human being is encompassed by his bodily dimensions, and his magnitude, commensurate with the appearance of his body, is the measure of his subsistence, so also, I think, that the entire plenitude of humanity was included by the God of all, by the power of his foreknowledge, as in one body, and that this is what the account teaches, saying that "And God made the human being, in accordance with the image" of God "made he him." . . . The human being manifested together with the first formation of the world, and he who shall come to be after consummation of all, both likewise have this: they equally bear in themselves the divine image. For this reason, the whole was called one human being, because to the power of God nothing has either passed or is to come, but even that which is looked for is embraced equally with the present by his all-embracing activity. The whole nature, then, extending from the first to the last, is a kind of single image of He Who Is. (*De hom.* 16.16–18)

The unity of all human beings—past, present, and future—as one human being is an expression of God's instantaneous and comprehensive act of making, which unfolds through its own sequence and order. There is, however, an important difference between how the beginning and the end are described: although both bear the divine image, it is only manifested at the beginning but comes to be at the end, after the consummation of all, that is, when the entire plenitude of human beings has been attained. Here we see the significance of the fact that Gregory has *not* been speaking of

Adam, who only appears in Genesis 2: Adam might be the first (the *protos*), but he is not the source, head, or beginning (the *archē*). The image of God, in accordance with whom God makes the human being in Genesis 1:27, is, as we saw earlier (*De hom.* 16.8), Christ Jesus, the Prototype, the one who comes to be at the end, after the consummation of all, "the entire fullness of humanity" foreseen by God from or in the beginning. Or, as Balthasar put it more elegantly: "The total Christ is none other than the total humanity."[8] Thus, human existence as male and female is not a secondary characteristic added in view of a "fall" into sin; rather, this is, when properly understood (and hence the "exercises" Gregory provides), the way in which the entire pleroma of humanity is attained. After all, as Gregory points out a little later, it is only after making the human being male and female that God blessed them to "increase and multiply" (*De hom.* 22.4; Gen 1:28). Foreseeing this plenitude of human beings, Gregory adds, God also foreknew "the time coextensive with the formation of human beings," so when the fullness had been attained, time itself should stop and "then should take place the reconstitution of all, and with the changing of the whole, humanity should also be changed, from the corruptible and earthy to the impassible and eternal" (*De hom.* 22.5–6), for as Paul affirmed: "We will all be changed" (1 Cor 15:51). And so, Gregory urges, as had Irenaeus, that we need patience. Let the one who complains about the burden of this life "await the time necessarily co-extensive with human increase" (*De hom.* 22.7), as did the patriarchs who also waited, for as Hebrews puts it: "God having foreseen something better for us, that without us they would not be made perfect" (Heb 11:40).

Having given these two analyses of the human being as the image of God, Gregory then turns in the final chapter to a full medical and anatomical analysis of an actual human being, just as does Timaeus in the last part of his discourse, where he attempts, as he puts it, "to put a final head on my story" (*Tim.* 69b1). Using ancient medical theory, Gregory describes how a seed is deposited in a womb, where the fetus grows by the power of growth and nutrition; then, when sufficiently formed and strong, the infant emerges into the world of sense-perception, where it continues to grow bodily—and now, also, in its reasoning faculty—recapitulating the stages of the evolution of the soul as Gregory reads Moses' anthropogony in Genesis 1. Allowing himself to be diverted into innumerable details, Gregory eventually recalls that his purpose was to show that "from animated and living

---

8. Balthasar, *Presence and Thought*, 87.

bodies, a being, living and animated from the first, is generated, and that human nature takes it and cherishes it, like a nursling, with her own powers" so that it grows appropriately in each part, "for it immediately displays, by this artistic and scientific process of formation, the power of the soul interwoven with it, appearing at first somewhat obscurely, but afterwards increasing in radiance concurrently with the perfecting of the organism" (*De hom.* 30.29).

Gregory then goes on to compare this process to that of a sculptor: intending to produce the figure of an animal in stone, the sculptor first separates the stone from its quarry, then chips away the superfluous parts, proceeding through the various steps of the first outline, when even an inexperienced observer can conjecture what the final figure will be, and then, working again at the material, until "producing in the material the perfect and exact form, he brings his art to its conclusion," and what had been shapeless stone is now a perfect figure of a lion or a human, "not by the material being changed into the figure, but by the figure being wrought upon the matter" (*De hom.* 30.30). In the same way, Gregory proposes,

> we say that nature, the all-contriving, taking from the kindred matter within herself the part that comes from the human being, crafts the statue. And just as the form follows upon the gradual working of the stone, at first somewhat indistinct but more perfect after the completion of the work, so also in the carving of the organism the form of the soul, by the analogy, is displayed in the substratum, incompletely in that which is incomplete, and perfectly in that which is perfect; but it would have been perfect from the beginning had nature not been maimed by evil. For this reason, our sharing in that impassioned and animal-like coming-into-being brings it about that the divine image does not shine forth immediately in the moulded figure, but, by a certain method and sequence, through those material and more animal-like attributes of the soul, brings to perfection the human being. (*De hom.* 30.30)

In speaking of "nature" being "maimed by evil," Gregory is not referring to a "fall" and corruption of human nature: here it is nature as an active force ("the all-contriving") that has been hindered. If the analogy with sculpting is to hold, then it would be the waywardness of the human will or the hardness of stoney hearts that hinders the work of nature in sculpting human beings, much like Timaeus's "straying cause," which needs to be "persuaded" by intellect. The concluding words in this passage are particularly striking: it is not simply by our "sharing in the impassioned and animal-like coming-into-being" that the human race reaches the plenitude foreseen by God (cf. *De hom.* 22.4), but that this entails that the human being is brought to perfection in a proper order and sequence. As Gregory now adds, this happens "*through* those more material and animal-like attributes of the soul." It is through the body and its sense-perceptive faculties, shared with other animals, that the human being "becomes rational" (cf. *De hom.* 10.1). If it is, as Gregory earlier argued, "the evil husbandry of the intellect" that has perverted all the motions and impulses shared with the other animals into forms of passion not known amongst the animals, then it is the intellect which needs training, to raise all these motions so that they, too, are "conformed to the beauty of the divine image" (*De hom.* 18.4–5) and the beauty of the divine image in the moulded figure can truly shine forth.

As with Irenaeus, Gregory uses the stages of human growth to understand the economy of God bringing about his project, to make a human being in his image and likeness. Gregory does this, as we have seen, through three coordinated analyses of the human being as the image of God: firstly, the ideal picture of the human being (chapters 1–15); secondly, an analysis of the prevision and provision of God with respect to the wavering inclination of the human will, sketching out the economy, or the "anthropogony," traced in the ascent of nature to the more perfect form of life, on the one hand, and, on the other hand, leading to the completion of the plenitude of the human race as the image of God, the total Christ, a process that requires, and is co-extensive with, time itself, resulting in the final transformation proclaimed by Paul (chapters 16–29); and finally, how the economy thus described is recapitulated in the life of each human being, from the seed being implanted in the womb and growing there through the power of nutrition, then coming into the world of sense-perception, where it continues to grow in both body and soul, learning discernment by experience and growing in virtue. And so, Gregory concludes his treatise with the exhortation, using Paul's words, that it is now time to put away childish things, the old human being, and put on the one being renewed in accordance with the image of God instead (*De hom.* 30.33; Col 3:9–10).

Gregory does not, in this treatise, go beyond urging putting off the old human and putting on the new, to consider what the final state of the human being will be, and, specifically, the place of sexuality within this. The most he has done is to note that although existence as male and female is the "particularities of human nature" and, indeed, the manner by which the human race attains to the plenitude of its calling, there is neither male and female in Christ. However, in his short work, *On Those Who Have Fallen Asleep*, Gregory does address the transformation that comes about through death and resurrection. Those displeased by this forthcoming transformation are, he says, like those who would prefer to remain as embryos in the womb, "for since the birth-pangs of death serve as the midwife assisting the birth of humans to another life, when they go forth to that light and draw in the pure Spirit, they know by experience what a great difference there is between that life and the present one, while those left behind in this moist and flabby life, since they are simply embryos and not humans [ἔμβρυα ὄντες ἀτεχνῶς καὶ οὐκ ἄνθρωποι]," call the departed "unhappy."[9] Just as in the case of a newborn infant, "an eye is opened for him when he leaves what now afflicts him," and also the other spiritual senses—hearing (quoting 2 Cor 12:4), taste (Ps 33:9), smell (2 Cor 2:14), and touch (1 John 1:1). And so, Gregory asks, "If these and such things are stored up for humans after the birth through death [τὸν διὰ τοῦ θανάτου τόκον], what is the purpose of grief, sorrow, and dejection"?[10] He then continues:

> Nature always trains us by death [ἐμμελετᾷ τῷ θανάτῳ] and death has been made to grow together with life as it passes through time. For since life is always moved from the past to the future and never does away with what follows afterwards, death is what always accompanies the life-giving activity by being united with it. For in the passing of time every life-giving movement and activity certainly ceases. Since, then, impotence and inactivity are the special property of death, and certainly this always follows after the life-giving activity, it is not outside the truth to say that death has been woven together with life. . . . That is why, according to the words of the great Paul, "we die daily" (1 Cor 15:31), not remaining constantly the same in the same house of the body, but, from time to time, we become different from something else, by addition and subtraction, being constantly changed as though to a new body [οὐχ οἱ αὐτοὶ διὰ παντὸς ἐν τῷ αὐτῷ διαμένοντες οἴκῳ τοῦ σώματος ἀλλ' ἑκάστοτε ἄλλοι ἐξ ἄλλου γινόμενοι, διὰ προσθήκης τε καὶ ἀλλοιούμενοι]. Why, then, are we astonished at death when the life existing through the flesh has been demonstrated to be its constant care and its training ground?[11]

---

9. *Mort.* [Heil, 47; Greer, 104–5].
10. *Mort.* [Heil, 47; Greer, 105].
11. *Mort.* [Heil, 52–53; Greer, 107–8].

With regard to the final transformation that will be effected when our desire returns again to God, Gregory begins by urging that "since the craftsman of the universe will at the appropriate time forge the lump of the body into a 'weapon of good pleasure' [Ps 5:13], 'the breastplate of righteousness' as the apostle says, and the 'sword of the Spirit' and the 'helmet' of hope, and the whole armor of God [Eph 6:14–17], love your own body [ἀγάπα τὸ ἴδιον σῶμα] according to the law of the apostle who says 'no one has hated his own body.'"[12] But if, as Paul says, we will have a "house not made by hands, eternal in the heavens" (2 Cor 5:1), a worthy "dwelling place of God in the Spirit" (Eph 2:22), how can that be described physically in the way our present state of embodiment can be described?

> Let no one describe to me the mark, shape, and form of that house not made with hands according to the likeness of the characteristic marks that now appear to us and that distinguish us from one another by special properties. For since it is not only the resurrection that has been preached to us by the divine oracles, but also that those who are being renewed by the resurrection pledged by divine Scripture must be changed [cf. 1 Cor 15:51], it is entirely necessary that what we shall be changed to has been hidden from absolutely everyone and is unknown, because no example of what is hoped-for is to be seen in the life we now live.[13]

The heaviness of the body as we now experience it will be transformed for those "whose elements of their bodies have been changed to a more divine condition" in which "there will be one kind for all when all of us become one body of Christ, having been shaped by one characteristic mark," so that "since the divine image shines equally on all, as to what will become ours in the change of nature instead of such properties we shall appear to be something better than any thought can guess."[14]

Maximos the Confessor

For Irenaeus and Gregory, as we have seen, the divine economy maps the growth towards the fullness of being human to which we are called, thus completing the divine project announced by God in the opening chapter of scripture. The end of the growth within the life-span of the human being

---

12. *Mort.* [Heil, 61–62; Greer, 113]; cf. Eph 5:29.
13. *Mort.* [Heil, 62; Greer, 113].
14. *Mort.* [Heil, 62–63; Greer, 114].

is the mystery of transformation spoken of by Paul (1 Cor 15:51), through which we come to "receive the power of the Uncreated" (*Haer.* 4.38.3). As Irenaeus put it, in a formula that became a dictum thereafter, "Our Lord Jesus Christ through his transcendent love became what we are that he might bring us to be even what he himself is" (*Haer.* 5.pr). That "God stands in the congregation of Gods" (Ps 82:1/81:1) refers, for Irenaeus to "the Father and the Son and those who have received adoption" (*Haer.* 3.6.1); we are to become "Gods," though this first requires that we become human (cf. *Haer.* 4.39.2).

That the end of the arc of the divine economy is set from the beginning is emphatically reaffirmed several centuries later by Maximos the Confessor. Addressing the question posed by Thalassios, asking how it can be that God "in the coming ages will show his riches" (Eph 2:7) and yet that "the end of the ages have come upon us" (1 Cor 10:11), Maximos begins his response with an all-encompassing programmatic statement:

> He who by the sheer inclination of his will established the *genesis* of all creation, visible and invisible, before all ages and before the very *genesis* of things that came to be, had an ineffably good plan [βουλήν] for them, which was for him to be mingled, without change, with the nature of human beings through a true union according to hypostasis, uniting to himself human nature, without alteration, so that, on the one hand, he would become human, in a manner he himself knows, and, on the other, he would make the human being God by union with himself, clearly dividing the ages wisely and determining some for the activity of him becoming human and others for the activity of making the human God. (*Ad. Thal.* 22.2)

In dividing the "ages" this way, between those devoted to God becoming human and those for the human to be made God, Maximos does not refer the former to the Old Testament and the latter to the New, or any such division, but rather offers three explanations for how there can be "coming ages" when "the end of the ages" has already arrived. The "ages" are, he starts, to be distinguished "conceptually [τῇ ἐπινοίᾳ]," and he offers as a first suggestion that "some are set aside of the mystery of the divine inhumanization and others for the grace of human divinization [τοὺς μὲν τῷ μυστηρίῳ τῆς θείας ἐνανθρωπήσεως, τοὺς δὲ τῇ χάριτι τῆς ἀνθρωπίνης θεώσεως]," the former are for "God's descent to humans, the latter belong to the ascent of the humans to God," and while the former have reached their proper end, the latter have not yet arrived (*Ad. Thal.* 22.5). "Or rather," Maximos continues, as Jesus Christ is "the beginning, middle, and end of all ages past, present, and future, one could say that through the power of faith 'the end of the ages'—that end which will be actualized by grace according to its proper form in the divinization of the worthy—'has already come upon us'" (*Ad. Thal.* 22.6). "Or alternatively," Maximos finally suggests in his third and fullest account, the two ages are distinguished as "the active and passive principles" (τὸν τοῦ ποιεῖν καὶ τοῦ πάσχειν λόγον): the present life is characterized by activity, for as the scripture puts it, "the human toiled in this age and shall live unto its end" (LXX Ps 48:10), whereas "the future ages of the Spirit, which will come about after this present life, are those of the transformation in passivity [τῆς τοῦ πάσχειν εἰσὶν μεταποιήσεως]" (*Ad. Thal.* 22.7). That is, our ability to act will come to an end (we will die), bringing the age of activity to a close and inaugurating the coming age. In this future age, Maximos continues:

> we shall passively undergo by grace the transformation of divinization [τὸ πάσχοντες τὴν πρὸς τὸ θεοῦσθαι χάριτι μεταποίησιν], no longer being active but passive, and for this reason we will not cease from being divinized [οὐ λήγομεν θεουργούμενοι]. For then, passivity will transcend nature, having no principle limiting the infinite divinization of those who passively experience it. For we act to the extent that our power of reason, which by nature is productive of the virtues, is active within us, and the power of the intellect, which by potential is unconditionally receptive of all knowledge, passes through the whole nature of beings and whatever can be known, and leaves behind itself all the ages. And we are passive when, having completely traversed the inner principles of beings created out of nothing, we will have come, in a manner beyond knowledge, to the Cause of beings, and, since all things will have reached their natural limits, our potentials for activity appropriate to them will come to rest. And we will become the very thing that is not in any way the outcome of our natural capacity, since nature does not possess the capacity to grasp what is beyond nature. For nothing created is by its nature capable of actualizing divinization, since it cannot grasp God. For this is the property of divine grace alone, that is, to grant the gift of divinization proportionately to created beings, brightly illumining nature by a light that transcends nature, actively elevating nature beyond its own proper limits through the excess of divine glory. (*Ad. Thal.* 22.7)

Our exertions in this age of activity—the life-span of a human being—are directed to the acquisition of virtue and knowledge, as our mind traverses all that can be known within nature. But beyond this activity is the transformation that is worked upon us when, no longer active but inactive (dead), we are fully passive and so able to be passively transformed. Called to this divine transformation from before even coming-into-being, human nature is thus receptive or "capable" of becoming "Gods," but only passively, as something that it cannot achieve of itself. On the other hand, while this transformation in passivity belongs to the age to come, the activity of present age is for the acquisition of virtue and knowledge. Regarding, then, the apparent contradiction between the two verses, Maximos concludes:

> As such, then, it does not seem that "the end of the ages had come upon us," since we have not yet received, by that grace that is in Christ, the gift of the good things that transcend the ages and nature, of which the mode of the virtues and the principles of those things that can be known by nature have been established as types and foreshadowings, through which God always wills to become human in the worthy. Blessed, then, is the one who, after making God human in himself through wisdom and fulfilling the *genesis* of such a mystery, passively becomes, by grace, God, for the fact of eternally becoming this shall have no end. (*Ad. Thal.* 22.8)

Thus, the present age, the life-span of each human being as active agents, is that in which God is "humanized," for "God always wills to become human in the worthy." Moreover, this "humanization of God" in each human being through virtue is a foreshadowing of the "divinization" belonging to the age to come. There is then a reciprocity between the humanization of God and the divinization of the human, between the active principle and the passive: the acquisition of virtue is active, but it is one in which we learn to become (actively) passive (taking up the cross of Christ), until, through our own death, we are finally and fully passive in the hands of God, who can now fully and finally be the Creator.[15]

---

15. See also, *Ambig.* 7: "The essence of every virtue is the one Logos of God, and this can hardly be doubted since the essence of all the virtues is our Lord Jesus Christ, as it is written 'God made him our wisdom, our righteousness, our holiness, and our redemption' [1 Cor 1:30]. . . . Having completed his course, such a person becomes God, receiving from God to be God [καθ' ὃν γίνεται Θεός, ἐκ τοῦ Θεοῦ τὸ Θεὸς εἶναι λαμβάνων]. . . . In honouring these principles and acting in accordance with them, he places himself in God alone throughout his entire being, so that he himself by grace is and is called God, just as God by his condescension is and is called human for the sake of the human, and so that the power of this reciprocal disposition might be shown forth therein, a power that divinizes the human through his love for God and humanizes God through his love for the human. And by this beautiful exchange, it renders God human by reason of the divinization of the human, and the human God by reason of the inhumanization of God. For the Logos of God (who is God) wills always and in all things to accomplish the

The most fascinating text of Maximos dealing with the role of death, or rather its "use" and "conversion" by Christ, is *Responses to Thalassios* 61. This time, he is responding to the question raised by Thalassios regarding two other verses from scripture (1 Pet 4:17–18; Prov 11:31): "What is the meaning of the phrase 'the time has come for judgment to begin from the house of God' and 'if the righteous human is scarcely saved'"? Maximos begins his response by describing how it is that pain has been affixed to pleasure:

> When God crafted the nature of human beings, he did not co-create with it sense-perceptive pleasure and pain, but a certain capacity for pleasure according to the intellect, by which [the human] would be able to enjoy him ineffably. Together with coming into being [ἅμα τῷ γενέσθαι], the first human, by sense-perception, gave this capacity—the natural desire of the intellect towards God—to things of sense-perception, activating, in the very first movement [κατ' αὐτὴν τὴν πρώτην κίνησιν], an unnatural pleasure through the medium of sense-perception. Being, in his providence, concerned for our salvation, God therefore affixed pain alongside this sensible pleasure as a kind of punitive faculty, whereby the law of death was wisely implanted in our corporeal nature to curb the folly of the intellect moving desire, against nature, toward sense-perceptible things. (*Ad. Thal.* 61.1)

Maximos is clearly not thinking of a temporal "fall," at some remote and distant past, but rather how the very first movement of the natural desire of our intellect is towards things of sense-perception themselves rather than through such things, towards God.[16] This initial, indeed "originating," movement results in a cycle of pleasure and pain that is ultimately

---

mystery of his embodiment" (PG 91.1081c–84d; Constas, 103–7). See also *Ambig.* 10: "They say that God and the human are paradigms of one another, so that as much as the human, through love, has divinized himself, to that same extent God is humanized for the human by his love for humankind" (PG 91.1113b; Constas, 165)."

16. One can perhaps think of this in terms of how Gregory described the way in which the infant, having grown by the power of nutrition in the maternal womb, emerges into the world of sense-perception, where both body and soul are to grow further, not only in stature but also now needing to learn discernment through experience, and especially coming to learn that what appears to be good is not the true criterion for what is good, so as to attain proper intellectual understanding. See further: *Mort.* [Heil, 48; Greer, 105]: "For since the perfect power of the soul is still not contained in the infantile body, while the operation of the senses is born immediately perfect together with the baby, because of this, reasoning in judging of the good is prejudged by sense-perception and what already appears to the senses is also supposed to be good."

pedagogical, resulting in "the expulsion of pleasure contrary to nature but not its complete eradication" (*Ad. Thal.* 61.3). This cycle of pleasure and pain, for Maximos, is rooted in the overturning of the proper relationship between "toil" and pleasure: the first human being, set in the garden to "work" in it (Gen 2:15), enjoyed the pleasure before undertaking any "toil," and so, to rectify the "debt" that thus occurred, "it was necessary that there be devised an unjust and likewise uncaused toil and death... so that a most unjust toil and death... would do away completely with the unrighteous beginning in pleasure as well as the consequent just end of nature through death" (*Ad. Thal.* 61.3–4), and this, of course, is Christ's own death (cf. "Who for the joy set before him endured the cross," Heb 12:2). In doing so,

> by giving our nature impassibility through his Passion, relief through his toils, and eternal life through his death, he restored [our nature], renewing its capacities by means of what was negated in his own flesh, and through his incarnation [σαρκώσεως] granting it that grace which transcends nature, by which I mean divinization. (*Ad. Thal.* 61.6)

In his passion, Christ thus reverses the path taken by Adam, which "introduced into nature another *archē* of *genesis*, constituted by pleasure but ending through toils in death," and so Christ "gave our nature another beginning of a second *genesis*, which through toil ends in the pleasure of the life to come" (*Ad. Thal.*, 61.7). As such, Christ has converted death itself: having had "pleasure as a mother," death now "becomes the father of eternal life" (*Ad. Thal.* 61.7). Moreover, when the Lord "naturally willed to undergo death itself in the passibility of his human nature—clearly suffering—he converted the use of death [τὴν τοῦ θανάτου χρῆσιν ἀντέστρεψεν], so that henceforth in him death would no longer be a condemnation of nature but clearly of sin" (*Ad. Thal.* 61.10). In this way, "the baptized"—that is, those who conform themselves to Christ's death (cf. Rom 6:3)—also "acquires the use of death to condemn sin, which in turn mystically leads that person to divine and unending life" (*Ad. Thal.* 61.11). By contrasting what happens in Adam and in Christ in this way, Maximos can utilize the contrast we saw in the preceding chapters between our original *genesis* and the new possibility of *gennēsis*: scripture distinguishes, he says, between "how the *genesis* from Adam accompanied by pleasure, in tyrannizing nature, was providing food for the death that arose in consequence of that pleasure," and, on the other hand, "how the *gennēsis* of the Lord in the flesh, which came about because his love for humankind, eliminated both these things," that is, Adamic pleasure and death (*Ad. Thal.* 61.8). And it is in these terms that Maximos can answer the question posed by Thalassios:

> That is, it was not possible for the *genesis*—which was in no way touched by that *archē* whose end was death—to be conquered in the end by corruption through death since, as I said, the *logos* has distinguished these things from one another, because for as long as our nature was being tyrannized solely by the characteristic marks of Adam in its beginning and end, by which I mean *genesis* and corruption, it was "not the time for the judgment" enabling the complete condemnation of sin "to begin." But when the Word of God appeared to us through the flesh and became perfect human but without sin, and in the flesh of Adam willingly bore only the punishment of Adam's nature, and when he "condemned sin in the flesh," innocently suffering as "righteous for the sake of the unrighteous," and converted the use of death, reworking it into the condemnation of sin but not of nature, then, I say, "it was time for the judgment to begin," a judgment consistent with this conversion of death [τὴν ἀντιστροφὴν τοῦ θανάτου] and leading the condemnation of sin. (*Ad. Thal.* 61.8)

Essential to this "reversal of death" or converting "the use of death" is the change from passivity to activity. When Maximos states that the coming-into-being (*genesis*) from Adam is accompanied by pleasure, it is important to recognize that his focus is not at all upon the parents and any pleasure, sinful or otherwise, they might experience in the act of procreation: the pleasure in question is that of the person coming into existence, a pleasure, moreover, that is not preceded by any work or toil. Our nature is "tyrannized solely by the characteristic marks of Adam in its beginning and end," that is, *genesis* and corruption or death. But that cycle is now broken by the work of Christ, who underwent the "toil" of the passion prior to any pleasure or joy, so converting death from being a passive end to an active beginning, or birth, for all who follow him.

One of the most striking texts of Maximos is *Ambiguum* 41, describing the path to be traversed by the human being. Maximos opens this text by asserting that "the existence [ὑπόστασιν] of all things that have come into being" is distinguished by five divisions: created/uncreated, intelligible/perceptible, heaven/earth, paradise/inhabited world, and finally, "the fifth is that according to which the human being who is above all—like a most capacious workshop containing all things and naturally mediating through itself all the divided extremities, having been placed amidst beings according to *genesis* [κατὰ γένεσιν]—is divided into male and female" (*Ambig.* 41.1–2). Maximos seems to be playing upon the word "*genesis*," referring both to how the human being comes to be and also to the book that relates this. Mediating between all these extremities, the human being has the potential and vocation to bring them all into unity and so "establish clearly through itself the great mystery of the divine goal [τοῦ θείου σκοποῦ]" (*Ambig.* 41.2). These divisions, thus, are not the result of a "fall" but rather the God-given structure and framework for the vocation of the human being. Indeed, the created world as described in the opening chapter of Genesis does in fact come about by God "separating" the various elements prior to the introduction of the human being.

Maximos follows this vision of divinely appointed cosmological divisions by tracing the path to be traversed in bringing all things into unity. The first step for humans is to begin with their own division. This is to be accomplished, according to Maximos, by

> completely shaking off from nature, by means of a supremely dispassionate condition of divine virtue, the property according to the female and the male, which clearly in no way depends [μηδαμῶς ἠρτημένην δηλαδή], according to the foregoing account [or "the guiding principle": κατὰ τὸν προηγούμενον λόγον], upon the divine purpose concerning the *genesis* of the human being [τῆς περὶ τὴν γένεσιν τοῦ ἀνθρώπου θείας προθέσεως], so that it might be shown to be, and becomes, simply a human being according to the divine purpose [ὥστε δειχθῆναί τε καὶ γενέσθαι κατὰ τὴν θείαν πρόθεσιν ἄνθρωπον μόνον], not divided by the designation according to the male and the female, in accordance with the principle by which it primarily came to be, nor divided into the parts that now appear around it, thanks to the perfect union, as I said, with its own principle, according to which it exists. (*Ambig.* 41.3)

The divine purpose, referred to twice here, is that stated in Genesis: the human being should come to be.[17] As such, the words translated as "the foregoing account" could refer back to Maximos's own account of the divisions found in creation, with the human being set the task of reconciling

---

17. Most translations render the clause τῆς περὶ τὴν γένεσιν τοῦ ἀνθρώπου θείας προθέσεως as "the divine purpose concerning human generation," or similar, that is, in terms of procreation and interpret it terms of the supposed teaching of Gregory of Nyssa about a two-stage creation and the possibility of multiplying sexlessly "as the angels." See Behr, *Gregory of Nyssa*, 133–34. Maximos, as we will see in *Ambig.* 41.7, is certainly able to speak directly about sexual intercourse when that is what he intends.

all things, bringing them into union and so establishing "the great mystery of the divine goal." Or they could refer to "the governing principle" of that divine purpose, which, as it concerns the vocation of the human being, is common to both male and female. If the divine purpose is to make a human being, with all that that entails (the vocation of overcoming divisions and bringing all things into unity with God), then the division into male and female "clearly in no way depends," as Maximos says, "upon the divine purpose concerning the *genesis* of the human being"; that is, this divine purpose does not require the division of the human being into male and female, even if it is a God-given division from which males and females must start in their coming to be a human being in accordance with the divine purpose. And this is to be achieved by the acquisition of divine virtue, so shaking off "the property according to female and male" and the removal of "the designation according to male and female" that currently divides the human being. Maximos perhaps reverses the usual order in the first instance to form a chiasm (female/male–simply human–male/female). Through this first mediation, then, "it is shown to be and becomes simply human [ἄνθρωπον μόνον] in accordance with the divine purpose."[18]

Maximos then continues by describing how the human being mediates between and unites the remaining divisions: paradise and the inhabited world, by a holy life; heaven and earth, by an identity of life with the angels through virtue; the intellectual and perceptible realms through knowledge; and finally, by "uniting the created nature with the uncreated through love (O the wonder of God's love for the human being!), the human being would show them to be one and the same by the state of grace, the whole [human being] being wholly interpenetrated by God and becoming everything that God is without the identity of essence, and receiving the whole God instead of itself" (*Ambig.* 41.4–5)

After describing how the human being did not accomplish the task set before it but rather overturned "the natural power to unite what was separated . . . for the division rather of what was united," Maximos then turns to Christ's work of unification. Christ initiates the universal union of all things with himself: "Beginning with our own division, he became

---

18. If Maximos is expounding, in his own way, the text of Genesis, then it is possible that in the phrase "only/simply human" (ἄνθρωπον μόνον) Maximos enigmatically hints towards Gen 2:18 (Οὐ καλὸν εἶναι τὸν ἄνθρωπον μόνον)—usually translated as "it is not good for man to be alone," but which could be translated as "it is not good to be only/simply human"—where this is the first and only thing said to be "not good." For this human life of virtue, see Costache, "Living Above Gender."

the perfect human [γίνεται τέλειος ἄνθρωπος]," like us in every way except sin (Heb 4:15), and "needing for this [i.e., becoming the perfect human] nothing of the natural process of marital intercourse" (*Ambig.* 41.7).[19] That Christ became human otherwise than through sexual procreation indicates, according to Maximos, the following:

> In this way, he showed, I think, that there was perhaps another mode, foreknown by God, for the growth to the multitude of human beings, had the first human kept the commandment and not cast himself down to the level of irrational animals by misusing the mode of his proper power, and so he drove out from nature the difference and division into male and female, which he in no way needed to become human, as I have said, and without which existence would perhaps have been possible; there is no necessity for these things to remain forever, for "in Christ Jesus," says the divine apostle, "there is neither male nor female" [Gal 3:28]. (*Ambig.* 41.7)

Maximos's point here is a counterfactual suggestion: God could "perhaps" have arranged things in such a way that the desired number of human beings was attained otherwise, for all things are possible for God, but he has in fact chosen for human beings the way in which we have come into existence. Most importantly, however, is that the way in which we "are shown to be and become simply human" is through the acquisition of virtue, so attaining the perfection of being human, as exemplified in Christ, is not the result of, nor does it even need, "the natural process of marital intercourse." The distinction between male and female is part of the framework established by God for the growth of the human being ("to be shown to be and become simply human"), but it is not needed to be human in the way that Christ has shown this to be—for this, virtue is needed.

Maximos continues by describing how Christ reconciled all the other divisions: uniting paradise and the inhabited world by his words on the cross to the thief, "Today you will be with me in paradise"; ascending into heaven with his body, so uniting heaven and earth; and passing beyond all the divine and intelligible ranks in heaven, so uniting the whole of creation. Regarding the final division, that between the uncreated and the created, Maximos says:

> And finally, after all these things, he—according to the concept of humanity—comes to be with God himself, "appearing on our behalf" as a human being, as it is written, "before the face of the God" and Father [Heb 9:24]—he who, as Word, can never in any

---

19. τῆς κατὰ τὴν φύσιν γαμικῆς ἀκολουθίας οὐδόλως εἰς τοῦτο προσδεηθείς.

> way be separated from the Father—fulfilling, as human, in deed and truth, with unwavering obedience, all that he himself, as God, had predetermined to take place, and perfecting the whole will of the God and Father for us, who had become useless by the misuse of the power naturally given to us from the beginning for this purpose. (*Ambig.* 41.9)

Maximos then immediately continues by recapitulating how Christ's work of unification is effected in us, beginning again from the division into male and female:

> Thus he united, first of all, ourselves in himself, through the removal of the difference according to the male and the female [τῆς κατὰ τὸ ἄρρεν καὶ τὸ θῆλυ διαφορᾶς], and instead of men and women [ἀντὶ ἀνδρῶν καὶ γυναικῶν], in whom this mode of division is especially evident [ἐνθεωρεῖται μάλιστα], he showed us as properly and truly to be simply human beings, thoroughly formed according to him, bearing his image intact and completely unadulterated, touched in no way by any marks of corruption. (*Ambig.* 41.9)

For the first time in this treatise, Maximos now speaks of "men and women" rather than "male and female," the latter being a division that is particularly seen in the former. What Maximos means by this is not quite clear, apart from the fact that he is evidently not equating "male and female" with "men and women," raising the question of whether he has even been talking about the latter in the previous passages.[20] As the sentence continues, its scope becomes ever more expansive with these striking words:

> And with us and through us the whole creation, encompassing the extremities through the intermediaries as through his own

---

20. Elsewhere in his writings, Maximos almost invariably takes "male and female" in a "spiritual" sense. For instance, in his *Commentary on the Our Father* he simply and directly takes the "male and female" of Gal 3:28 to indicate "ire and desire" (*Or. dom.* [Deun, 47; Berthold, 108]). When these contrary dispositions are put aside so that the *logos* is not enslaved by them, he continues, the divine image shines forth, remolding the soul to the divine likeness according to its will. In this way, "it comes to be in the great kingdom, subsisting essentially with the God and Father of all, as a radiant dwelling place of the Spirit, wholly receiving, if one may so speak, the power of the knowledge of the divine nature as far as possible," and it is in this way, finally, that "Christ always wills to be born mystically, becoming incarnate in those being saved, and rendering the soul begetting him to be a virgin mother, not having, to speak concisely, according to the comparison, as male and female, the properties of nature subject to corruption and *genesis*" (*Or. dom.* [Deun, 50; Berthold, 109]). For Maximos's cosmological understanding of "incarnation," see Wood, *Whole Mystery of Christ*.

members, and binding inseparably around himself, each with the other, paradise and the inhabited world, heaven and earth, the perceptible and the intelligible (since he has, like us, a body and perception and soul and mind), by which, as [his own] parts, individually assimilating the extremity of each to what is universally akin in the previously mentioned manner, "he" divinely "recapitulated all things in himself" [Eph 1:10], showing that the whole creation exists as one, like another human being [μίαν ὑπάρχουσαν τὴν ἅπασαν κτίσιν δείξας, καθάπερ ἄνθρωπον ἄλλον], being brought to perfection by the convergence of its own parts with each other and inclining towards itself by the wholeness of [its] existence, according to the one and simple and undefined and undifferentiated concept of its derivation from non-being, in accordance with which the whole of creation admits of one and the same absolutely undiscriminated *logos*, that non-being is prior to being. (*Ambig.* 41.9)

After giving a different analysis of the divisions and unity within creation, this time in terms of species and genus, Maximos concludes this work:

For the "wisdom" and the prudence of "the God" and Father is the Lord "Jesus Christ" [1 Cor 1:24, 30], the one holding together the universals of beings by the power of wisdom and embracing the parts from which they are completed by the prudence of understanding—since by nature he is the fashioner and provider of all things—and drawing through himself into one what is divided and dissolving the strife among beings and binding everything into peaceful friendship and undivided harmony, "both what is in heaven and what is on earth" [Col 1:15], as the divine Apostle says. (*Ambig.* 41.11)

In many ways, it is these final words, drawing upon Paul's words about the crucified one in Colossians, that provide the key for understanding the whole text. It is from the work of Christ, in particular in his passion, that Maximos derives the five-fold division within creation: the divisions that he sees within the whole of creation are the divisions that Christ has united, or, as Maximos put it, when completing his work and coming before the Father as a human being, he fulfills, as human, that which he, as God, predetermined to take place, so fulfilling the will of God and completing the great mystery (*Ambig.* 41.9). As such, what Maximos offers in this text is a fully Christocentric cosmology as well as anthropology, one, in fact, in which the whole cosmos is seen as "another human being."[21]

21. For other dimensions of Maximos's anthropological thinking, see *Myst.* 4 (where

Finally, Maximos follows Gregory of Nyssa's suggestion that we are but fetuses and not yet human, speaking, in a most striking manner, of the sense-perceptible world as a womb:

> For it is true—though it may be a jarring and unusual thing to say—that both we and the Word of God, the Creator and Master of the universe, exist in a kind of womb, owing to the present conditions of our life. In this sense-perceptible world, just as if he were enclosed in a womb, the Word of God appears only obscurely, and only to those who have the spirit of John the Baptist, while, on the other hand, human beings, gazing through the womb of the material world, catch but a glimpse of the Word who is concealed within beings (and this, again, only if they are endowed with John's spiritual gifts). For when compared to the ineffable glory and splendor of the age to come, and to the kind of life that awaits us there, this present life differs in no way from a womb swathed in darkness, in which, for the sake of us who were infantile in mind, the infinitely perfect Word of God, who loves mankind, became an infant. (*Ambig.* 6.3)

Both Gregory and Maximos take Paul's words in Romans 8 seriously (and literally!): The whole of creation is groaning in travail, awaiting the unveiling of the sons and daughters of God.

Reading scripture from the perspective of the end that is the pascha of Christ, Ireneaus, Gregory, and Maximos see the whole economy of God as bringing his creature, through growth in time, to come to be in the image and likeness of God and to share in the uncreated power of God. In their different ways, they present a very realistic picture, one that matches our concrete existence and experience: we do, in fact, all come to be passionately, on the part of our parents, as well as passively, on our part, into existence in time with a path of growth before us, which inexorably leads to death. But as our end is co-terminal with that of Jesus Christ, through the mystery of his pascha, our death can now be a voluntary and active birth into life as a human being in the image of God. For Irenaeus, this is mapped by the seven stages of human life; for Gregory, it reflects the dynamic power of nature, "the all-contriving," as it molds and shapes the creature, training it by death, to arrive at its end; while Maximos sees the path in cosmological terms, bringing the whole cosmos, "as another human being," into unity with God.

---

the church is seen as imaging the human being); *Myst.* 6 (how scripture is said to be a human being); and *Myst.* 7 (how the cosmos is called a human being and the human being is called a cosmos).

Postscript

Returning from the theological framework imposed by "The Bible" (Figure 1) to that which opens up with the unveiling of the scriptures (the "Old Testament") in the light of Christ's passion, it is striking how much more expansive the mystery of Christ becomes and how much more realistically the economy of God is described. The whole economy, Irenaeus argued, has been arranged in such a way "so that we should neither undervalue the true glory of God nor be ignorant of our own nature, but should know what God can do and what benefits the human, and so that we should never mistake the true understanding of things as they are, that is, of God and the human being" (*Haer.* 5.2.3). It is, in other words, either both real and true or neither.

 Carefully attending to the manner of reading scripture in the light of pascha, the transformation of death into life that this effects, and the way in which this (singular) paschal light gradually refracted over the early centuries into a spectrum of particular feasts and moments, with their iconographic depictions, each bearing the paschal imprint, we have found a very consistent understanding of the economy of God, the mystery of Christ, and the reality of being human. The paschal death of Jesus upon the cross is not taken as the mid-point of human history but rather as the end of the scriptural arc of the economy of God—from Adam to Christ, from animation by a mortal breath to the life-giving Spirit—an end that is coterminous, though not of course simultaneous, for all. The paschal mystery also contains within it, later refracted into a separate feast, the birth of the Lord Jesus Christ, the Son eternally begotten of, or taking his begetting from, God, as he lays down his life in an act of love, so being "the image of the invisible God" (Col 1:15) in whom the Father rejoices. As "the pioneer of our salvation," moreover, Jesus Christ is not only "the firstborn of the dead" but also "the firstborn of many brethren," for he has transformed the tomb, our common end, into the womb in which we can be born into life. Furthermore, the Lord Jesus who is the Christ is also the head of the body of Christ, and, as Ignatius observed, a head cannot be born without the members of the body in the birth to which he calls us through the cross, the birth of the whole body of Christ in whom the Father again rejoices, with the same joy.

Not only is the mystery of Christ truly universal and integrative in this manner, but the economy of God, the arc from Adam to Christ, is expounded in very realistic terms. Rather than speculating about a "pre-lapsarian Adam" falling from an initial perfection into mortality and corruption at some remote point in the past but infecting human nature thereafter, the way of thinking that we have traced sees a path of growth set before each human being and the human race as a whole. The time of scripture is, as we have seen, the present, in which we read scripture from beginning to end or dip in and out of various places, the time in which we grow from infancy to maturity, from Adam to Christ. And so the economy of God, as pedagogy, is understood in terms of growth, mapped, in various ways, by the concrete reality of our actual existence, whether the seven stages of life, as with Irenaeus, or the growing power of animation, as with Gregory. For we have all, in fact, come into existence passively, with a life of growth before us that necessarily terminates in death, and the path of growth traversed by the individual human does indeed seem to recapitulate that of the human race as a whole.[1]

This does not imply an initial lack of perfection, though that perfection, as with a newborn baby, is but an initial stage. Moreover, for an infant to grow necessarily involves falling: the infant will physically fall down while learning to walk, bruising the infant and causing sorrow to the parent who patiently stands by, "bearing with" the infant, as Irenaeus would put it, as they learn to walk, and so on, with different modalities, throughout the course of our lives, as we grow from Adam to Christ, until in the passivity and weakness of death we finally learn that the strength of God is made perfect in weakness (2 Cor 12:9). That the infant cannot immediately walk is not due to some primordial "fall," nor is it because the infant or the

---

1. LeCron Foster, "Symbolism," 386, notes that "both biological evolution and the stages in the child's cognitive development follow much the same progression of evolutionary stages as that suggested in the archaeological record."

parents sinned; rather, as Christ responded to such a question, "it is so that the works of God might be manifest in him" (John 9:3), as the man, blind from birth rather than by accident or illness, is made whole by Jesus' action of taking mud and spittle to fashion that which was lacking, recapitulating the way God is described as forming human beings in Genesis 2, so, as Irenaeus concludes, the work of God "is fashioning the human being" (*Haer.* 5.15.2). If "sin" (ἁμαρτία), however, is defined as "falling short of the mark," then from the beginning each has certainly fallen short of that to which we are called, but it is only by growing and learning that we reach that end. In the light of Christ we can see how far, individually and collectively, we have fallen short from the beginning, but we are also enabled to see our current situation pedagogically, as the "birth-pangs" of the children of God in the womb of this world (Rom 8). This approach doesn't minimize the reality, and horror, of the sinful and destructive world in which we live—about which we must mourn and protest, against which we must struggle—but it also knows that it is out of death that God brings life. In the same way that the sinful action of Joseph's brothers turns out, at the end of the account, to be God's own action in preserving life, so too the end of our life—death, now subsumed in the pascha of Christ—and the whole of our life, seen from the point of view of the transformative paschal end, is the economy by which all is brought into subjection to the head and the life that comes from him, the one who then hands over everything to God, who will in the end indeed be all in all (1 Cor 15:21–28).

Approached in this way, the church (not the buildings or the institutions that coordinate the activity of particular communities) is the virgin mother, who is figured in Mary as she receives the Gospel; it is in her womb that we are born into life by entering the paschal mystery. The church, as the local community, is also the body of Christ, a royal priesthood, in which each is the celebrant of the paschal mystery in and through their own lives, the mystery that is anticipated in baptism and eucharist. And, finally, the church is the spouse of Christ, being prepared to be the pure virgin to be united to her head, the Lord Jesus Christ (cf. 2 Cor 11:2; Eph 5:31–32; Rev 22:17), in the final eschatological marriage. In this sense the ecclesial communities are not so much those who are "called out" of the world but those who, in this world (the womb in which we grow), are already bearing witness to the renewed creation, as the first spring flowers appearing in the midst of the world whose form is passing away under the winter sun.

Finally, the age of our lives now, as we have seen Maximos expound it, is the age of activity, in which God becomes human in those acquiring virtue, whereas the age to come is characterized by passivity, in which the human becomes God. God and the human beings are, in his striking words, paradigms of one another; the humanization of God and the divinization of the human being are two reciprocal movements, turning upon the cross: individually, the first movement terminates with our death, but this end begins the second movement; collectively, the line of coming-into-being (*genesis*) terminates with Jesus Christ (as with the genealogy of Matthew), who, as the firstborn of the dead, begins the line of birth (*gennēsis*) which returns back to Adam, the Son of God (as with the genealogy of Luke), who is, as Origen concluded, Christ, or as Balthasar put it, "the total Christ is none other than the total humanity."[2] It is this end, no less, to which we are called and invited to voluntarily embrace in a priestly manner, even now, as we grow inexorably towards it. Death is both that which is universal, the natural correlate of coming-into-being (*genesis*), and intrinsically particular: no one can give it to me (I can be put to death, but it will be my death) nor take it away from me (someone can die in my place, but it will be their death not mine); it is, as Derrida points out, the only pure gift.[3] But the "conversion of the use of death" by Jesus Christ—from being something to which I am passively subjected to that which, in and by Christ, I can now "use" actively, by taking up the cross and following Christ—enables us to transform the ground of our existence from mortality and necessity to freedom and love: our "Let it be" or "Amen" to God's creative act, with the economy thus understood, now becomes an "I am."

What we have thus found when tracing the shape of (early) Christian theology is a remarkable union of theology and anthropology bound intrinsically together in a paschal Christology—if, indeed, these can be separated even "in thought alone." Premised upon the pascha of Jesus Christ and the conversion of death into birth that it effects, as proclaimed by the apostles in accordance with the scriptures, we are offered a way to understand the reality of the span of our life as the scriptural movement from Adam to Christ, individually and collectively, in a growth that culminates in the mystery of the transformation heralded by Paul (1 Cor 15:51–54).

If this approach to Christian theology strikes us as odd or different to that to which we have become accustomed, then that demonstrates how

---

2. Balthasar, *Presence and Thought*, 87.
3. See Behr, "Irenaeus' Gratitude and Derrida's Gift."

great a hold the theological framework of "The Bible" has had on our theological imaginations. But as C. S. Lewis pointed out, in his preface to the translation of Athanasius's *On the Incarnation*, it is only by reading the "old books" that we are able to have the "clean sea breeze blowing through our minds," breaking habits of thought that we no longer even recognize. This does not necessarily mean, he accepts, that they are right. Yet growing in understanding does necessarily mean seeing things otherwise than we currently do. As Lewis emphasizes, this means reading books by those outside our own era, and as the books of the future are unavailable to us, the path left to us is to approach again the old books, to think through the past so as to be able to think into the future.

Bibliography

Primary Sources

Alexander of Aphrodisias. *De Mixtione (Mixt.)*. In *Alexander of Aphrodisias: A Study of the De Mixtione with Preliminary Essays, Text, Translation, and Commentary*, edited and translated by Robert E. Todd. Philosophia Antiqua 28. Leiden: Brill, 1976.
Aristotle. *Rhetoric (Rhet.)*. Edited by W. D. Ross. Translated by G. A. Kennedy. OCT. 1959. Reprint, Oxford: Oxford University Press, 1991.
Athanasius. *Canons: The Canons of Athanasius of Alexandria*. Edited and translated by W. Riedel and W. E. Crum. 1904. Reprint, Amsterdam: Philo, 1973.
———. *Contra Gentes (Gent.)*. Edited and translated by Robert W. Thomson. OECT. Oxford: Clarendon, 1971.
———. *On the Incarnation (Inc.)*. Edited and translated by John Behr. PPS 44a. Crestwood, NY: St Vladimir's Seminary Press, 2011.
———. *Orations Against the Arians (C. Ar.)*. C. Ar. 1–2, edited by K. Metzler and K. Savvidis, fasc. 2. In vol. 1.1 of *Athanasius Werke*. Berlin: de Gruyter, 1998.
———. *Orations Against the Arians (C. Ar.)*. C. Ar. 3, edited by K. Metzler and K. Savvidis, fasc. 3. In vol. 1.1 of *Athanasius Werke*. Berlin: de Gruyter, 2000.
———. *Orations Against the Arians (C. Ar.)*. Translation in NPNF[2] 4.
Augustine. *The Confessions (Conf.)*. Translated by M. Boulding. Works of Augustine for the Twenty-First Century 1.1. New York: New City, 1997.
———. *On The Trinity (Trin.)*. Translated by E. Hill. Brooklyn, NY: New City, 1991.
Cabasilas, Nicholas. *Life in Christ*. Edited by M.-H. Congourdeau. Translated by C. J. deCatanzaro. Crestwood, NY: St Vladimir's Seminary Press, 1974.
Clement of Alexandria. *Paedagogue (Paed.)*. Edited by O. Stählin. Revised by U. Treu. GCS 12. 3rd ed. Berlin: Akademie Verlag, 1972. Translation in ANF 2.
———. *Stromata (Strom.)*. In *Strom. I–VI*. Edited by O. Stählin. Revised by L. Früchtel. GCS 52. 3rd ed. Berlin: Akademie Verlag, 1972.
———. *Stromata (Strom.)*. In *Strom. VII–VIII*. Edited by O. Stählin. Revised by L. Früchtel and U. Treu. GCS 17. 2nd ed. Berlin: Akademie Verlag, 1970.
———. *Stromata (Strom.)*. Translation in ANF 2.
Cyprian of Carthage. *On the Unity of the Church (Unit. eccl.)*. In *St Cyprian of Carthage On the Church, Select Treatises*. Translated by Allen Brent. PPS 32. Crestwood, NY: St Vladimir's Seminary Press, 2006.

Bibliography

Depositio Martyrum. In *Das Kalenderhandbuch von 354: Der Chronograph des Filocalus*. Edited by Johannes Divjak and Wolfgang Wischmeyer. Vienna: Holzhausen, 2014.

Egeria. *Egeria's Travels to the Holy Land*. Translated by John Wilkinson. Rev. ed. Jerusalem: Ariel, 1981.

Ephrem. *Commentary on the Diatessaron* (*Comm. Diat.*). Translated by Carmel McCarthy. Journal of Semitic Studies Supplement 2. Oxford: Oxford University Press, 1993.

———. *Commentary on Genesis* (*Comm. Gen.*). In *St Ephrem the Syrian: Selected Prose Works*, edited by K. McVey. Translated by E. G. Mathews and J. P. Amar. FC 91. Washington, DC: Catholic University of America Press, 1994.

———. *Hymns on the Crucifixion*. In *Des Heiligen Ephraem des Syrers, Paschahymnen (de azymis, de crucifixione, de resurrection)*, edited by Edmund Beck. CSCO 248. Scripores syri 108. Louvain: CSCO, 1964.

———. *Hymns on the Crucifixion*. In "Ephrem the Syrian's Hymn *On the Crucifixion* 4." Translated by Philippus J. Botha. *HTS Teologiese Studies/Theological Studies* 71.3 (2015). https://doi.org/10.4102/hts.v71i3.3012.

———. *Hymns on the Nativity*. In *Ephrem the Syrian: Hymns*. Translated by K. E. McVey. CWS. Mahwah, NJ: Paulist, 1989.

Eusebius of Caesarea. *Ecclesiastical History* (*Hist. Eccl.*). Edited and translated by K. Lake. LCL. 2 vols. Cambridge: Harvard University Press, 1989.

———. *Life of Constantine*. Translated Averil Cameron and Stuart Hall. Oxford: Oxford University Press, 1999.

The Festal Menaion. Translated by Mother Mary and Archimandrite Kallistos Ware. London: Faber and Faber, 1969.

Gregory of Nazianzus. *Oration* 31. In *Grégoire de Nazianze: Discours 27–31 (Discours Théologiques)*, edited and translated [French] by P. Gallay with M. Jourjon. SC 250. Paris: Cerf, 1978.

———. *Oration* 31. In *St Gregory of Nazianzus: On God and Christ: The Five Theological Orations and Two Letters to Cledonius*. Translated by L. Wickham and F. Williams. PPS 23. Crestwood, NY: St Vladimir's Seminary Press, 2002.

Gregory of Nyssa. *Against Eunomius* 3.3. In *Contra Eunomium libri*, edited by W. Jaeger, 107–33. Gregorii Nysseni Opera 2. 1960. Reprint, Leiden: Brill, 2002.

———. *Against Eunomius* 3.3. In *Gregory of Nyssa: Contra Eunomium III; An English Translation with Commentary and Supporting Studies: Proceedings of the 12th International Colloquium on Gregory of Nyssa (Leuven, 14–17 September 2010)*, edited by Johan Leemans and Matthieu Cassin, 106–21. Translated by Stuart G. Hall. Suppl. VC 124. Leiden: Brill, 2014.

———. *Against Eunomius* 3.3. Translation in NPNF[2] 5.

———. *Hexameron* (*Hex.*). Edited by Hubertus R. Drobner. GNO 4.1. Leiden: Brill, 2009.

———. *Hexameron* (*Hex.*). Translation by Robin Orton. FC Shorter Works 1. Washington, DC: Catholic University of America Press, 2021.

———. *On the Human Image of God* (*De hom.*). Edited and translated by John Behr. OECT. Oxford: Oxford University Press, 2023.

———. *On Those Who Have Fallen Asleep* (*Mort.*). Edited by Gunter Heil. GNO 9.1. Leiden: Brill, 1967.

———. *On Those Who Have Fallen Asleep* (*Mort.*). In *One Path for All: Gregory of Nyssa on the Christian Life and Human Destiny*, 94–117. Translated by Rowan A. Greer. Eugene, OR: Cascade, 2014.

Gregory Palamas. *Homilies*. Translated by Christopher Veniamin. Waymart, PA: Mount Thabor, 2009.

Bibliography

———. *Homilies*. Edited by B. Ψευτογκας. ΣΥΓΓΡΑΜΜΑΤΑ 6. Thessalonika: Kuromanos, 2015.

Grosseteste, Robert. *Cessation of the Laws*. Edited by R. C. Dales and E. B. King. Auctores Britannici Medii Aevi 7. London: British Academy/Oxford University Press, 1986.

———. *Cessation of the Laws*. Translated by S. M. Hildebrand. FC Mediaeval Continuation 13. Washington, DC: Catholic University of America Press, 2012.

Hermas. *The Shepherd* (Herm. *Vis.* and *Sim.*). Edited and translated by K. Lake. LCL Apostolic Fathers 2. Cambridge: Harvard University Press, 1976.

Hippolytus. *On the Christ and the Antichrist* (*Antichr.*). Edited by H. Achelis. GCS 1.2. Leipzig: Heinrichs Verlag, 1897. Translation in ANF 5.

Ignatius of Antioch. *Letters*. In *Ignatius of Antioch: The Letters*. Edited and translated by A. Stewart. PPS 49. Yonkers, NY: St Vladimir's Seminary Press, 2013.

Irenaeus of Lyons. *Against the Heresies* (*Haer.*). Edited and translated [French] by A. Rousseau et al. SC 100, 152–53, 263–64, 293–94, 210–11. 5 vols. Paris: Cerf, 1965, 1969, 1979, 1982, 1974. Translation in ANF 1.

———. *Against the Heresies* (*Haer.*). Translated by D. J. Unger. Revised by J. J. Dillon et al. 4 vols. ACW 55, 64, 65, 72. New York: Paulist/Newman, 1992, 2012, 2024.

———. *Demonstration of the Apostolic Preaching* (*Dem.*). In *Irenaeus of Lyons: On the Apostolic Preaching*. Translated by John Behr. PPS 17. Crestwood, NY: St Vladimir's Seminary Press, 1997.

John Chrysostom. *The Divine Liturgy*. Ἡ Θεία Λειτουργία τοῦ ἐν Ἁγίοις Πατρός ἡμῶν Ἰωάννου τοῦ Χρηνυστοστόμου/*The Divine Liturgy of Our Father Among the Saints John Chrysostom*. Text and translation by Ephrem Lash. London: Greek Orthodox Archdiocese of Thyateira and Great Britain, 2011.

———. Η ΘΕΙΑ ΛΕΙΤΟΥΡΓΙΑ—*The Divine Liturgy of St John Crysostom*. Oxford: Oxford University Press, 1995.

———. *Homilies on Matthew* (*Hom. Matt.*). PG 57. Translation in NPNF[1] 10.

Justin Martyr. *Dialogue with Trypho* (*Dial.*). Edited by Miroslav Marcovich. PTS 47. Berlin: de Gruyter, 1997. Translation in ANF 1.

Martyrologium Hieronymianum. In *Acta Sanctorum, Tomus II pars posterior*. Edited by H. Delehaye et al. Brussels: Bollandists, 1931.

The Martyrdom of Polycarp (Mart. Pol.). Edited and translated by Kirsopp Lake. LCL Apostolic Fathers 2. Cambridge: Harvard University Press, 1976.

The Martyrology of Tallaght. Edited and translated by Richard Irvine Best and Hugh Jackson Lawlor. London: Harrison and Sons, 1931.

Maximos the Confessor. *Ambigua* (*Ambig.*). In *On Difficulties in the Church Fathers: The Ambigua*. Edited and translated by Nicholas Constas. 2 vols. DOML. Cambridge: Harvard University Press, 2014.

———. *Commentary on the Our Father* (*Or. dom.*). In *Maximus Confessor: Selected Writings*, edited by George Berthold, 99–125. CWS. London: SPCK, 1985.

———. *Expositio orationis dominicanae* (*Or. dom.*). In *Opuscula exegetica duo*. Edited by Peter van Deun. CCSG 23. Turnhout: Brepols, 1991.

———. *Mystagogy* (*Myst.*). In *Saint Maximus the Confessor: On the Ecclesiastical Mystagogy*. Edited and translated by Jonathan Armstrong. PPS 59. Yonkers, NY: St Vladimir's Seminary Press, 2019.

———. *Responses to Thalassios* (*Ad. Thal.*). Edited by Carl Laga and Carlos Steel. CCSG 7, 22. Turnhout: Brepols, 1980, 1990.

Bibliography

———. *Responses to Thalassios* (*Ad. Thal.*). In *On Difficulties in Sacred Scripture: The Responses to Thalassios*. Translated by Maximos Constas. FC 136. Washington, DC: Catholic University of America Press, 2018.
The Mishnah. Translated by Herbert Danby. Oxford: Oxford University Press, 1933.
Origen. *Commentary on John* (*Comm. John*). Edited by Erwin Preuschen. GCS 10. Origenes Werke, 4. Leipzig, Hinrichs, 1903.
———. *Commentary on John* (*Comm. John*). Translated by R. E. Heine. FC 80, 89. Washington, DC: Catholic University of America, 1989, 1993.
———. *Homilies on Jeremiah* (*Hom. Jer.*). Edited by Erich Klostermann. Revised by P. Nautin. GCS 6. Origenes Werke 3. 2nd ed. Berlin, 1983.
———. *Homilies on Jeremiah* (*Hom. Jer.*). Translated by John Clark Smith. FC 97. Washington, DC: Catholic University of America Press, 1998.
———. *On First Principles* (*Princ.*). Edited and translated by John Behr. OECT. Oxford: Oxford University Press, 2017.
The Oxford Annotated Mishnah. Edited by Shaye J. D. Cohen et al. Oxford: Oxford University Press, 2022.
Plato. *Timaeus* (*Tim.*). Edited by J. Burnet. OCT, Platonis Opera, 4. Oxford: Clarendon, 1902.
———. *Timaeus* (*Tim.*). In *Timaeus*. Translated by Donald J. Zeyl. Indianapolis: Hackett, 2000.
Plotinus. *Enneads* (*Enn.*). Edited by Paul Henry and Hans-Rudolf Schwyzer. OCT, Plotini Opera. 3 vols. Oxford: Clarendon, 1964, 1977, 1983.
———. *Enneads* (*Enn.*). Translated by Lloyd P. Gerson. Cambridge: Cambridge University Press, 2018.
Ps. Ephrem. *Sermones in Hebdomadam Sanctam* (*Serm.*). Edited by Edmund Beck. CSCO 412; Scripores Syri 181. Louvain: CSCO, 1979.
Ps. Longinus. *On the Sublime*. Edited and translated by Stephen Halliwell. Oxford: Oxford University Press, 2022.
Quintilian. *Institutio oratoria* (*Instit.*). In *Quintilian: The Orator's Education*. Edited and translated by Donald A. Russell. LCL. Cambridge: Harvard University Press, 2001.
Second Epistle of Clement (2 Clem.). Edited and translated by Christopher Tuckett. OAF. Oxford: Oxford University Press, 2012.
Tertullian. *On the Soul* (*An.*). Edited by J. H. Waszink. Amsterdam: Mülenhoff, 1947. Translation in ANF 3.
Theophilus of Antioch. *To Autolycus* (*Autol.*). Edited and translated by R. M. Grant. OECT. Oxford: Oxford University Press, 1970.
Victorinus. *On the Making of the World*. Edited and translated [French] by M. Dulaey. SC 423. Paris: Cerf, 1997.

Modern Sources

Anatolios, Khaled. *Athanasius: The Coherence of His Thought*. London: Routledge, 1998.
Banev, Krastu. "Myriad of Names to Represent Her Nobleness: The Church and the Virgin Mary in the Psalms and Hymns of Byzantium." In *Celebration of Living Theology: A Festschrift in Honour of Andrew Louth*, edited by Justin A. Mihoc and Leonard-Daniel Aldea, 75–103. London: Bloomsbury, 2015.
Barr, James. *Garden of Eden and the Hope of Immortality*. Minneapolis: Fortress, 1992.

Bibliography

Barth, Karl. *Christ and Adam: Man and Humanity in Romans 5*. Introduction by Wilhelm Pauck. Translated by T. A. Smail. New York: Collier, 1962.

Balthasar, Hans Urs von. *Presence and Thought: An Essay on the Religious Philosophy of Gregory of Nyssa*. Translated by Mark Sebanc. San Francisco: Ignatius, 1995.

Behr, John. *The Nicene Faith*. Crestwood, NY: St Vladimir's Seminary Press, 2004.

———. *Irenaeus of Lyons: Identifying Christianity*. CTC. Oxford: Oxford University Press, 2013.

———. *John the Theologian and His Paschal Gospel*. Oxford: Oxford University Press, 2019.

———. "One God Father Almighty." *MTh.* 34.4 (2018) 320–30.

———. "Our Mother Church: Mary and Ecclesiology." *IJSCC* 22.4 (2022) 333–44.

———. "Irenaeus' Gratitude and Derrida's Gift: Time, Death, Life." *Philosophy, Theology and the Sciences* 9.1 (2022) 5–21.

———. "'For This Reason the Father Loves Me': Drawing Divinity into Himself to Minister Divinity to Us." *IJST* 25.1 (2023) 47–59.

———. "Speaking of Incarnation: Modern Predicaments and Ancient Paradigms." *IJST* (forthcoming).

Brent, Allen. *Hippolytus and the Roman Church in the Third Century: Communities in Tension Before the Emergence of a Monarch-Bishop*. Suppl. VC 31. Leiden: Brill, 1995.

Briggman, Anthony. "Literary and Rhetorical Theory in Irenaeus, Part 1." *VC* 69 (2015) 500–527.

———. "Literary and Rhetorical Theory in Irenaeus, Part 2." *VC* 70 (2016) 31–50.

Brock, Sebastian P. "Mary and the Gardener: An East Syriac Dialogue Soghitha for the Resurrection." *Parole de l'Orient* 11 (1983) 223–34.

———. *Mary and Joseph, and Other Dialogue Poems on Mary*. Texts From Christian Antiquity 8. Piscataway, NJ: Gorgias, 2011.

Brown, Raymond. *An Adult Christ at Christmas: Essays on the Three Biblical Christmas Stories Matthew 2 and Luke 2*. Collegeville, MN: Liturgical, 1978.

———. *The Birth of the Messiah: A Commentary on the Infancy Narratives in the Gospels of Matthew and Luke*. Anchor Bible Reference Library. New ed. New York: Doubleday, 1993.

Chapman, John. "Papias on the Age of Our Lord." *JTS* 9 (1907) 42–61.

Chupungo, Anscar J. *The Cosmic Elements of Christian Passover*. SA 72. Rome: Anselmiana, 1977.

Constas, Maximos. *The Art of Seeing: Paradox and Perception in Orthodox Iconography*. Los Angeles: Sebastian, 2014.

Costache, Doru. "Living Above Gender: Insights from Maximus the Confessor." *JECS* 21.2 (2013) 261–90.

Crossan, John Dominic, and Sarah Sexton Crossan. *Resurrecting Easter: How the West Lost and the East Kept the Original Easter Vision*. New York: HarperOne, 2018.

Dalferth, Ingolf U. *Crucified and Risen: Restructuring the Grammar of Christology*. Grand Rapids: Baker Academic, 2015.

Évieux, P. "La Théologie de l'accoutumance chez saint Irénée." *RSR* 55 (1967) 5–54.

Gambero, L. *Mary and the Fathers of the Church: The Blessed Virgin Mary in Patristic Thought*. Translated by T. Buffer. San Francisco: Ignatius, 1999.

Giulea, Dragoş Andrei. "Apprehending 'Demonstrations' from the First Principle: Clement of Alexandria's Phenomenology of Faith." *JR* 89.2 (2009) 187–213.

Bibliography

Gockel, Matthias. "A Dubious Christological Formula? Leontius of Byzantium and the Anhypostasis–Enhypostasis Theory." *JTS* NS 51.2 (2000) 515–32.

Gore, Charles. *Lux Mundi: A Series of Studies in the Religion of the Incarnation*. London: John Murray, 1889.

Greer, Rowan A. "The Man from Heaven: Paul's Last Adam and Apollinarius' Christ." In *Paul and the Legacies of Paul*, edited by W. S. Babcock, 165–82, 358–60 (endnotes). Dallas: Southern Methodist University Press, 1990.

Hart, Addison Hodges. *The Woman, the Hour, and the Garden: A Study of Imagery in the Gospel of John*. Grand Rapids: Eerdmans, 2016.

Hays, Richard B. *Echoes of Scripture in the Letters of Paul*. New Haven, CT: Yale University Press, 1989.

Henry, Michel. *I Am the Truth: Towards a Philosophy of Christianity*. Translated by Susan Emanuel. Cultural Memory in the Present. Stanford, CA: Stanford University Press, 2003.

Hick, John. *God and the Universe of Faiths: Essays in the Philosophy of Religion*. London: Macmillan, 1973.

———, ed. *The Myth of God Incarnate*. London: SCM, 1977.

Janeras, Sebastia. *Le Vendredi-Saint dans la Tradition Liturgique Byzantine*. SA 99/ Analecta Liturgica 13. Rome: Pontificio Ateneo S. Anselmo, 1988.

Jervis, L. Ann. *Paul and Time: Life in the Temporality of Christ*. Grand Rapids: Baker Academic, 2023.

Johnson, Maxwell E. "Martyrs and the Mass: The Interpolation of the Narrative of Institution into the Anaphora." *Worship* 87.1 (2013) 2–22.

Kartsonis, Anna D. *Anastasis: The Making of an Image*. Princeton, NJ: Princeton University Press, 1986.

Lampe, Peter. *From Paul to Valentinus: Christians at Rome in the First Two Centuries*. Minneapolis: Fortress, 2003.

LeCron Foster, Mary. "Symbolism: The Foundation of Culture." In *Companion Encyclopedia of Anthropology: Humanity, Culture, Social Life*, edited by Tim Ingold, 366–95. London: Routledge, 1993.

Leithhart, Peter. *Revelation 1–11*. International Theological Commentary. London: Bloomsbury/T&T Clark, 2018.

Levison, John R. *Portraits of Adam in Early Judaism: From Sirach to 2 Baruch*. Journal for the Study of the Pseudepigrapha, Supplement Series 1. Sheffield, UK: Sheffield Academic, 1988.

Lieu, Judith. "The Mother of the Son in the Fourth Gospel." *JBL* 117.1 (1998) 61–77.

Lossky, Vladimir. *The Mystical Theology of the Eastern Church*. Cambridge: James Clarke, 1957.

Louth, Andrew. "Inspiration of the Scriptures." *Sobornost* 31.1 (2009) 29–44.

———. "Mary the Mother of God and Ecclesiology: Some Orthodox Reflections." *IJSCC* 18.2–3 (2018) 132–45.

———, ed. *The Oxford Dictionary of the Christian Church*. 4th ed. Oxford: Oxford University Press, 2022.

Lubac, Henri de. *The Motherhood of the Church*. San Francisco: Ignatius, 1982.

Machabée, Stéphanie. "Life and Death, Confession and Denial: Birthing Language in the Letter of the Churches of Vienne and Lyons." In *Coming Back to Life: The Permeability of Past and Present, Mortality and Immortality, Death and Life in the Ancient Mediterranean*, edited by Frederick S. Tappenden and Carly Daniel-Hughes,

Bibliography

287–308. Montreal, QC: McGill University Library, 2017. http://comingbacktolife.library.mcgill.ca.

Martyn, J. Louis. "John and Paul on the Subject of Gospel and Scripture." In *Theological Issues in the Letters of Paul*, 209–30. Studies of the New Testament and Its World. Edinburgh: T&T Clark, 1997.

Mengozzi, Alessandro. "A Sureth Version of the East-Syriac Dialogue Poem of Mary and the Gardener." *Kervan: International Journal of Afro-Asiatic Studies* 23 [Special Issue] (2019) 155–74.

Mroczek, Eva. *The Literary Imagination in Jewish Antiquity*. Oxford: Oxford University Press, 2016.

Nautin, Pierre. *Lettres et écrivains chrétiens des IIe et IIIe siècles*. Paris: Cerf, 1961.

Pannenberg, W. "Christologie und Theologie." In *Grundfragen systematischer Theologie*, 129–45. Gesammelte Aufsätze II (198). Göttingen: Vandenhoeck & Ruprecht, 1980.

Radde-Gallwitz, Andrew. "Contra Eunomium III 3." In *Gregory of Nyssa: Contra Eunomium III; An English Translation with Commentary and Supporting Studies: Proceedings of the 12th International Colloquium on Gregory of Nyssa (Leuven, 14–17 September 2010)*, edited by Johan Leemans and Matthieu Cassin, 293–312. Suppl. VC 124. Leiden: Brill, 2014.

Rahner, Hugo. *Mater Ecclesia: Lobpreis der Kirche aus dem ersten Jahrtausend*. Köln: Benziger, 1944.

Roll, Susan K. *Toward the Origins of Christmas*. Liturgia condenda 5. Leuven: Peeters, 1995.

Rowland, Christopher, and Christopher R. A. Morray-Jones. *The Mystery of God: Early Jewish Mysticism and the New Testament*. Leiden: Brill, 2009.

Schmemann, Alexander. *The Eucharist*. Crestwood, NY: St Vladimir's Seminary Press, 1988.

Schniedewind, William M. *How the Bible Became a Book*. Cambridge: Cambridge University Press, 2004.

———. *Who Really Wrote the Bible: The Story of the Scribes*. Cambridge: Cambridge University Press, 2024.

Shults, F. LeRon. "A Dubious Christological Formula: From Leontius of Byzantium to Karl Barth." *TS* 57 (1996) 431–46.

Skinner, Quentin. "Meaning and Understanding in the History of Ideas." In *Regarding Method*, 57–89. Vol. 1 of *Visions of Politics*. Cambridge: Cambridge University Press, 2002.

Spronk, Klaas, et al. *Catalogue of Byzantine Manuscripts in Their Liturgical Contexts*. Subsidia 1, *Challenges and Perspectives*. Turnhout, Belgium: Brepols, 2013.

Stang, Charles. "Origen's Theology of Fire and the Early Monks of Egypt." *MTh*. 38.2 (2022) 338–62.

Steenberg, M. C. "Children in Paradise: Adam and Eve as 'Infants' in Irenaeus of Lyons." *JECS* 12.1 (2004) 1–22.

Stewart, Alistair. *The Original Bishops: Office and Order in the First Christian Centuries*. Grand Rapids: Baker Academic, 2014.

Talley, Thomas J. *The Origins of the Liturgical Year*. 2nd ed. Collegeville, MN: Liturgical, 1991.

Varalis, Yannis D. "The Nativity of Christ on Late Antique Ivories." *After Constantine* 1 (2021) 55–67. www.afterconstantine.com.

Wood, Jordan Daniel. *The Whole Mystery of Christ: Creation as Incarnation in Maximus Confessor*. Notre Dame, IN: University of Notre Dame Press, 2022.

Yarbrough, Robert W. *The Salvation Historical Fallacy: Reassessing the History of New Testament Theology*. History of Biblical Interpretation Series 2. Leiden: Brill, 2004.

Zumstein, Jean. "Intratextuality and Intertextuality in the Gospel of John." In *Anatomies of Narrative Criticism: The Past, Present, and Futures of the Fourth Gospel as Literature*, edited by Tom Thatcher and Stephen D. Moore, 121–36. Atlanta: SBL, 2008.

Index of Ancient Sources

I: SCRIPTURE

Genesis

1:26	71
1:27	74, 102–5
1:28	95, 106
2	71–72
2:8	72
2:15	115
2:24	69
3:20	71
45:4–5	17

Exodus

4:22	66
12–13	47 n.28
15:21	84

Deuteronomy

14:1	66
32:5	66
32:19	66

1 Kgdms (1 Sam)

2:6	16, 20

Psalms

2:7	56, 62
19:5/18:6	73
45:2–4/44:3–5	77
45:7/44:8	60, 61, 7
48:10 (LXX)	112
50:6/49:6	77
82:1/81:1	111
82:6–7/81:6–7	65, 100
104:29–30/103:29–30	90
110:1/109:1	76

Proverbs

8:22–25	56
8:25	62
8:30–31	63
8:31	66
11:31	114

Wisdom of Solomon

1:13	20

Isaiah

6:1	76
7:14	77
8:3	77
9:6	77
10:22–23	11
43:6	66
52:13—54:1	47–48, 69–70, 78
53:8 LXX	77

Index of Ancient Sources

Jeremiah
2:19 — 97
17:9 — 77
31:9 — 66

Daniel
7:13 — 76

Hosea
13:14 — 22

Zechariah
12:10 — 77

Malachi
4:1 — 77

Matthew
1:1 — 23
1:18 — 23
3:12 — 77
12:49–50 — 83
13:55 — 83
25:41 — 77

Mark
6:3 — 83
10:18 — 62
10:38 — 89

Luke
1:46–55 — 82
3:17 — 77
3:28–38 — 23
8:21 — 83
12:49 — 62
17:33 — 16
18:8 — 77
23:53 — 70
24 — 10

John
1:13 — 80
1:14 — 66
1:18 — 66
2:1–4 — 71
3:3 — 65
3:16 — 65, 66
3:18 — 66
6:14 — 82
8:57 — 99
9:3 — 125
10:10 — 16, 71 n.4
10:17 — 64
12:32 — 44
14:9–10 — 64
15:13 — 65
16:21 — 71–72
17 — 65
19:3 — 96
19:5 — 71
19:25–27 — 82
19:26 — 72
19:30 — 64
19:30 — 71
20:15 — 72

Acts
2:23–24 — 17
2:24 — 47
2:36 — 62
13:32–33 — 56, 62

Romans
1:2–4 — 43
2.28–29 — 22–23
5:3–5 — 80
5:12–14 — 19–22
5:12 — 71
5:14 — 13, 94
6:1–11 — 48
6:3–11 — 70
6:5 — 89
6:11 — 89
8 — 122, 125
8:18–32 — 66
8:29 — 48, 80, 93

Index of Ancient Sources

8:32	66
9:28	11
10:17	68
12:5	48
13:9	11
16	91
16:25–27	7

1 Corinthians

1:23	34
1:24	121
1:30	121
4:15	68
10:11	111
10:18	22
12–13	48
12:13	48
12:27	48, 68
13:8	66
15	12–22
15:3–5	7
15:13	43–44
15:21–22	15
15:28	66, 90
15:45–49	14, 94
15:47	14
15:51–54	126
15:51	106, 110, 111
15:56	22

2 Corinthians

1:22	96
4–5	7
5:1	110
11:2	69, 73
12:9	67, 101, 124

Galatians

3:28	102, 104, 119
4:1–3	47
4:4	26, 47, 68, 81
4:5–7	47
4:19	68
4:22–27	47
4:24–26	69

Ephesians

1:4	26
1:10	11, 121
1:13	90
1:14	96
1:22–23	69
2:7	111
2:22	110
4:13	16, 26
5:32	69

Philippians

2:6	61, 64, 95
2:8	61, 64, 88

Colossian

1:15	64, 65, 121, 123
1:18–19	69
1:18	24, 47, 48, 65, 80, 93
1:20	64
2:9	61, 69
2:19	48
3:9–10	108
3:15	68

1 Thessalonians

2:7	68
2:11	68

2 Thessalonians

1:6–8	77
1:9–10	77

Hebrews

2:10	93
2:14–15	22
4:15	119
9:24	119
10:1	27
11:40	106
12:2	115

Index of Ancient Sources

1 Peter
2:9	89
4:17–18	114

1 John
3:8–9	62
4:7	65
4:8	66

Revelation
1:5	47, 93
3:14	47, 93
21:2	73

2: OTHER ANCIENT SOURCES

Aristotle
Rhet 3.14.1	49

Athanasius
C.Ar.
1.15.4	57
1.15.6	57
1.16	57–58
2.2.6	56
2.82.2–3	63–64

Gent.
1	4, 32–33, 36

Inc.
1	33
8–9	34–35
8	37
10	35
16	36
19	36
25	37
27	37
31	37
32	37
54	37 n.17

Canons of Athanasius
16	45 n.22

Augustine,
Conf.
11.17–28	26
11.33	27

Trinity
4.2.9	54

Cabasilas Nicholas
Life of Christ
6.92–94	13

Cassian, John
Conference
10.2.1	45 n.22

Chrysostom, John
Hom. Matt. 44
	83

Clement of Alexandria
Paed.
1.6.41.3–42.2	74

Strom.
6.15.125.3	10
7.16.95.4–6	10

2 Epistle of Clement
14	73–74

Cyprian
Unit. eccl.
5–6	75–76

Index of Ancient Sources

Depositio martyrum   45

Ephrem
Comm. Diat.
12.5   82

Crucifixion
4.17   82

Ps–Ephrem
Serm,
7, 192–97   83

Eusebius of Caesarea
Life of Constantine
4.36   2 n.6

Eccl. Hist.
5.1–4   67–68
5.1.18–19   67
5.1.41–42   67
5.1.45–46   46, 68

Gregory the Theologian
Or.
31.8   57

Gregory of Nyssa
De hom.
4–5   102
7   102
8:4–7   101
9.1   101–2
10.1   102, 108
16.7–18   102–6
18.4–5   108
22.4   106, 108
22.5–6   106
22.7   106
30.29   106–7
30.30   107
30.33   108

Hex.
64   103

Mort.
    109–10
    114 n.16

Hermas
Sim.
8.7.4–6   91

Vis.
1.2.1   73
2.4.1   73
3.3.3   73
3.9.7   91
4.2.1   73

Hippolytus,
Antichr.
4   74–75
61   74

Ignatius
Rom.
4.1   89
6   46

Trall.
11.2   48

Eph.
20.2   89

Index of Ancient Sources

Irenaeus

Haer.

1.8–9	9
3.6.1	111
3.10.2	82, 84
3.20.1–2	97
3.22.3–4	24
3.22.3	94
3.22.4	80–81
3.24.1	90
4.4.1	21, 95
4.4.3	95
4.5.1	95
4.11.1	95
4.14.2	95
4.20.7	96
4.20.8	11
4.26.1	8
4.26.2–33.15	76
4.33.4	78
4.33.9–10	76
4.33.9	78
4.33.11–14	76
4.33.11	76–77
4.33.12–15	77
4.34.1	11
4.37–39	96–100
4.38.3	111
4.39.2	111
5.Pr	111
5.1.3	15, 94
5.2.3	100–101
5.2.3	123
5.8.1	90
5.9.2	96
5.16.2–3	95
5.12.1–2	15–16
5.15.2	125

Ps-Longinus,

On the Sublime

1.4	10

Martyrology of Jerome   49

Mart. Pol.

15.2	89

Maximus the Confessor

Ad Thal.

22	111–13
61	46 n.27
61	114–16

Ambig

6	122
7	113 n.15
10	113 n.15
41	116–21

Commentary on the Our Father

	120 n.20

Myst.

4	121 n.21
7	121 n.21

Mishnah,

Hagigah

2.1	18

Origen

Hom. Jer.

9.4	62–63

Comm. John

1.26	27
1.37	27
1.38	27
1.39	27
1.45	27
1.231	64
2:17–18	59
10.229	37–38
32.325–26	61

Index of Ancient Sources

Princ.

1.2.10	56
1.2.13	62
2.6.6	60–61
3.6.3	66
4.3.6–7	22–24

Gregory Palamas

Hom.

37	85

Plato

Timaeus

47e4	101 n.6
48a2–3	101 n.6
69a7–b12	101 n.6
69b1	106

Plotinus

Enn.

3.7.11, 43	27

Quintilian

Instit.

6.1.1	11
7.10.14–17	9

Tertullian

An.

43.10	71

Victorinus of Pettau

De Fabrica mundi

9	99

Index of Authors

Anatolios, K., 32 n.8
Apollinarius, 14
Athanasius, 3–4, 32–38, 45, 55, 56–58, 58 n.37, 63–66

Balthasar, H. U. von, 106, 126
Banev, K., 85 n.17
Barr, J. 5, 20–21
Barth, K., 13–14
Behr, J., 46 n.26, 57 n.35, 58 n,37, 62 n.40, 71 n.3, 5, 76 n.9, 91 n.27, 28, 94 n.1, 101 n.6, 117 n.17, 126 n.3
Brent, A. 45, n.23
Briggman, A., 9 n.16
Brock, S., 72 n.6
Brown, R., 49, 84
Bulgakov, S., 89

Cabasilas, N., 13
Chapman, J., 99 n.4
Chupungo, A. J., 49 n.30
Clement of Alexandria, 10
Chrysostom, John, 83
Constas, M., 85–86, 87–88
Costache, D., 118 n.18
Crossan, J. D., 43–44

Dalferth, I., 29–32, 37, 38, 48, 49, 55–56, 126,

Évieux, P., 16 n.26, 96 n.3

Galadza D., 70 n.2
Giulea, D. A., 10
Gore, C., 29
Gockel, M., 30 n.8
Greer, R. A., 14 n,24
Gregory of Nyssa, 62, 101–10, 124
Gregory Palamas, 85
Gregory the Theologian, 57
Grosseteste, R., 22

Hart, A. H., 71 n.4
Hays, R. B., 9
Henry, M., 46 n.26
Hick, J., 29
Hofmann, J. C. von, 12

Ignatius, 124
Irenaeus, 7–8, 10, 19, 76–78, 94–101, 124

Janeras, S., 70 n.2
Jervis, L. A., 18–20
John the Evangelist, 70–72
Johnson, M., 89 n.26

Kartsonis, A. D., 42 n.20

Lampe, P., 91 n.27
LeCron Foster, M., 124 n.1
Leithart, P., 72
Levison, J., 4
Lewis, C. S., 127
Lieu, J., 71 n.5

Index of Authors

Lossky, V., 88
Louth, A., 2 n.6, 89 n.25
Lubac, H. de, 88

Machabée, S., 46 n.26
Martyn, J. L., 9
Maximos the Confessor, 110–22, 126
Melito of Sardis, 10
Mengozzi, A., 72 n.7
Morray-Jones, C. R. A., 18 n.28
Mroczek, E., 1–2

Nautin. P., 67 n.1

Origen, 22–24, 27–28, 56–57, 58–63, 126

Pannenberg, W., 30 n.8
Pauck, W., 14
Paul the Apostle, 68–70

Radde-Gallwitz, A., 62 n.40
Rahner, H., 88

Roll, S., 45
Rowland, C., 18 n.28

Schmemann, A., 27 n.42
Schniedewind, W., 3 n.8
Shults, F. L., 30 n.8
Spronk, K., 2 n.7
Stang, C., 62 n.39
Steenberg, M. C., 16 n.27, 95 n.2
Stewart, A., 91 n.27

Talley, T., 4, 38, 45 n.22, n.23

Varalis, Y. D., 50 n.34
Victorinus of Pettau, 99

Wood, J. D., 120 n.20

Yarbrough, R. W., 12 n.19

Zumstein, J., 49

www.ingramcontent.com/pod-product-compliance
Lightning Source LLC
Chambersburg PA
CBHW061942220426
43662CB00012B/1993